# START ME UP

Tips, Tales, and Truths about
**Starting Up** *and*
**Starting Over**

**Jeannie Edmunds**

The stories in this book reflect the author's recollection of events. Some names, locations, and identifying characteristics have been changed to protect the privacy of those depicted. Dialogue has been recreated from memory.

The author is not a medical professional or a therapist. None of the advice in this book is meant to guide anyone toward or away from any medication, treatment, or physical activity.

Start Me Up ©2021 by Jeanne Edmunds Ringe

Published in the United States by FoxRaven Publishing
www.foxraven.net

ISBN (paperback): 978-0-578-91013-0
ISBN (ebook): 978-0-578-92228-7

Publication date: June 21, 2021

Book design: David Provolo
Author Photo: Scott R. Kline

Special discounts for bulk sales. Please contact the publisher.

Reviews welcome and appreciated!

*For everyone who has tried and failed and didn't give up,*
*and for everyone who wishes they could be that brave.*

*And for my two loves, Margaret and Dave, who inspire me,*
*challenge me, and make my life interesting enough to write about.*
*I promise I'll never write another book,*
*unless I get a big, fat advance.*

# Start Me Up Advance Praise

"How many start-up books have some of us read over the years? (I've authored fourteen of them.) But this one above all the rest makes me smile and want to read every word, as much for Jeannie's wisdom as for her stories. Even the most experienced of us can learn from our contemporaries, which Jeannie proves again and again with each uniquely named chapter. You've gotta read this!"

**Dave Berkus**, *Super angel investor and author of "The Berkus Method" of valuing early stage companies*

"As a psychotherapist, a coach, and the mother of a successful entrepreneur, I can unequivocally state that Jeannie has all the qualities which make her an expert in the entrepreneurial mindset: Optimism, resilience, courage, and a strong belief in her strengths and abilities. I could not put the book down once I started it."

**Andrea Siegman**, *Marriage and Family Therapist*

"I learned early on that it takes more courage to leave an unfulfilling work situation than it does to stay. However, there wasn't an instruction manual. With *Start Me Up*, Jeannie has provided the tools and tips necessary to pivot successfully. The desire isn't enough. Be prepared to roll up your sleeves and get to work—and bring along a highlighter!"

**Mara Gordon**, *Founder, Aunt Zelda's*

"Jeannie provides wisdom with a fresh perspective on how one should view their lives and careers. While challenging many of the assumptions on how to start a new career or restart after failure, after reading this book, you can only feel that anything is possible. As Jeannie stresses, successful people do the things they don't want to do because they know they should. That simple truth unlocks huge opportunities for all readers."

**Tig H. Krekel**, *Former Aerospace CEO, Serial Entrepreneur in Multiple Industries*

# **Start Me Up** Advance Praise

"While we've known Jeannie first as a mentor for starting a new business, through this book, we've gotten a window into her extraordinary life. Her incredible intuition and insight, for both business and beyond, now make total sense. Her advice and wisdom is woven through her life stories in this fun and fast read. Whether you're thinking of starting a company, starting a new job, or just need a life re-set, you will be inspired!"

**Shaz Rajashekar**, *Co-Founder, Shaz & Kiks*

"At Modern Elder Academy we encourage people to do what they're called to do. Clearly *Start Me Up* is what Jeannie was meant to create and share with the world, to inspire others to reinvent themselves, as she has, and to do it successfully."

**Chip Conley**, *Hotelier, Author, Speaker*

"Great fun and full of useful insights. I had a hard time putting it down."

**Ryan Abbott**, *MD, JD, PhD, Author, "The Reasonable Robot: Artificial Intelligence and the Law"*

"Inspirational, motivating, and useful . . . Jeannie Edmunds has written a must-read for anyone considering a leap into the startup world."

**Matthew Iommi**, *Co-CEO, Fetii, Inc.*

"What Jeannie Edmunds and *Start Me Up* reminds us of, that is critical to a world in need of the truly new, is that each of us is only limited by our own aperture of possibility. And that we are the ones who determine how wide that aperture is open by how willing we are to step into what that quantum field of potential is putting in front of us. Jeannie has done that again and again to literally become living proof that anything is possible for us. We just have to start."

**Kirk Souder**, *Leadership Coach + Founder, Enso Impact Agency*

# Contents

# Foreword

As the owner of Expert DOJO, the fastest growing startup accelerator in Southern California and the gateway to the rest of the world, I have the privilege of investing in and supporting hundreds of companies. Over the course of a year, I will assess and review up to 1,000 companies in my search for the perfect unicorn. Finding that billion-dollar breakthrough company is as much an art as it is a science, but we start every day with that goal in mind.

When we look for future unicorns to invest in, we look at five main areas. The first is the execution power of the founder. Success leaves clues. Then we look at the team's skill gaps, which is as much for today as it is for the future. What are the necessary skills required for this company to scale very fast and what is missing in this team? The fewer the gaps, the better the odds of success. The third area for us is to be able to see a straight line to the startup achieving $100,000 per month in revenue or an equivalent in users if the company is user-focused. Jeannie will be the first to tell you that only four percent of all companies in the USA hit $100,000 a month in revenue so it has to be clear to see. Then we want to know that the market size can support a 10-million-a-month company. This is also very important, as only one in a hundred of that four percent hit 10 million a month. Finally, we want the founder to be an exceptional money raiser. This is a high bar for all you startups but one that is a necessary for you—and for you to get our attention!

When we invest in startups, we believe that we must also educate and prepare them for the battles ahead. We are lucky to have Jeannie among the exceptional trainers we rely on at Expert DOJO to lift our startups to the required level. Our startups always get so much from her sessions. To be successful as a startup you must be a warrior and understand that you will come out the other side of the startup journey a different person. Although very few make it to the finish line, those who do experience a sense of true purpose that few others will experience. That feeling is worth every step of the journey.

My final piece of advice to all startups is that the investment is not the objective. You have three battles at any one time. One is to grow your company, another is to get an investment, and the final one is against time. Always fight time first. If you beat time, then the investment will follow. Grow fast and build the foundation as you scale. There is so much more to learn about starting a company, or starting anything in life, even if you're starting over after being knocked down a peg or two. You are in good hands with Jeannie to learn it all in this book.

God speed to you all.

—Brian McMahon

# Author's Note

Following my career path is like trying to catch a cricket with a pair of chopsticks. I've never landed in one place, one job, one life situation for very long. This has satisfied my deep curiosity and drive to continually educate myself. Acquire new skills. Keep trying new things. If I were more focused and, frankly, adept at office politics, I could have been coasting in upper management with a nice pension by now. But I have a low tolerance for boredom and bureaucracy.

So, I'm my own employer, with the attendant risks and rewards of an entrepreneurial life. Today, as Startup Jeannie, I advise entrepreneurs who are starting companies, most you haven't heard of—yet. I get referrals for new clients by word of mouth. No advertising. Satisfied clients and continual networking keep me in business.

My career is a long-simmering jambalaya: a spicy stew of tasty learning opportunities, sweet surprises, satisfying endings, and exciting beginnings.

I have been a writer. Radio talk show producer, network TV producer, and on-camera reporter. A documentary filmmaker. Book editor. Product developer. Spanish-to-English interpreter. Legislative aide. Magazine editor. Direct marketer. A salesclerk, and a pro shop manager. Partner in an infomercial company, and part of a food startup. Fundraiser for a non-profit. Director of a public-private partnership for the Library of Congress. I am also a late-in-life mom, a divorcee, and a widow. And I'm one of the lucky few who hit the jackpot on a dating app. In my 60s. I've lived in Asia, South America, and Europe. New York, DC, Austin, LA, and San Francisco. All the cool places. I've changed addresses every three to four years since I left my small town in the South to attend a big university in Texas.

I grew up in a close-knit family, but my charmed adult life has been occasionally shattered by family members' struggles with anxiety, depression, and addiction. Along the way I had to become an expert in medical insurance, rehab, and the type of brain cancer that killed my husband in 2016.

But we all have our sh*t, don't we? I won't burden you too much with mine. I just wanted to let you know that I understand the struggle.

I'm only sharing stories that are interesting, cautionary, and entertaining. Stories from my life, and the lives of those who have influenced me. My goal is to inspire you. To encourage you to review your own strengths and weaknesses as you read about mine, and as you prepare for and undergo your own reinventions.

Whether you find something to emulate in my experiences or not, with every goal you set for yourself, I encourage you to reach way up, beyond what you think you're capable of. Let your dreams define you. Not your history.

Pompous business books bore me. I promise you won't be bored.

I've tried to write this book as if we were having a conversation. I'm sharing some of my deepest secrets and vulnerabilities at the speed my brain works, which is kind of fast: You may have to put the book down and take a breath here and there.

So how will you decide if you're ready to start up or start over? You will know, in your gut, by the time you've finished this book. These are big life decisions. I know. That's why you're here, looking for help.

Startup Jeannie is here to help start you up.

Jeannie
Llano, Texas
2021

# Introduction
## Ending Up in Startups

I love startups. Here's why.

People who start companies are creative and courageous. Most of the entrepreneurs I've met, advised, consulted for, and mentored are superheroes. I feel such affection for them; it's as if I had birthed them myself. Whether it's a 17-year-old with an idea he's testing or an adult who's using her life savings to build her new company, they're all my progeny.

Startup founders learn to confront their fears and suppress their inner and outer critics as they ride the rapids of contradictory opinions about their businesses. This is true when they first get started as well as when they've already begun their journey. No kidding, this is one of the hardest things you must do as an entrepreneur: Figure out the difference between advice that sounds good and good advice. Staying true to the vision and mission is essential to a startup's success.

Staying mindful helps, too. As my entrepreneurial hairdresser, Lori, says, "I meditate. It's a bad neighborhood inside my head. You don't want to go there without a weapon. Meditation protects me. And my faith protects me."

God, I love Texans!

Lori tells me she had a loyal and sizable high-end clientele at a big-city beauty parlor before she decided to start over in her own salon in tiny town Texas. Her professional skills, attention to detail, and staying true to her vision have made her successful. She sets her own schedule, and her appointment book is nearly always full. Two years after she opened her doors, she has a waiting list for appointments.

Founders sometimes think they need a multi-million-dollar idea, a breakthrough product, a "killer app." They simply need to set out to solve a problem, disrupt a market, or develop something people didn't even know they needed until it was invented. Then they must execute exceptionally well, which is the hard part. All of this takes ovaries (or balls) of steel. Having a team of experienced startup advisors and mentors certainly helps.

Most, a big percentage, the vast majority, okay, *almost all startups fail.* Imagine how courageous founders have to be, knowing *that* before they even begin. As a wise investor once told me: Ideas are plentiful. They are *the what.* Show me *the how, the who, and the why.*

Even with all the boxes checked it's still a crapshoot, but investors know that. They also know that if they're very careful when calculating the risks, one of their bets might pay off with a nice "exit."

**Working in startups can give you a chance to use your skills to help build something from the ground up. You'll wear many hats, working side by side with people who can teach you things. Have you considered starting over by starting your own business?**

Don't dismiss the idea yet. We're just getting started.

My decade in Startup Land has been exhilarating and rewarding. I may be an immigrant here (after careers in other fields) but I'm legit: I've helped start three companies with two to four other people:

▲ An online diet program for kids, which launched and then shut down in the first year;

▲ A music-based startup that moved back to London, downsized, and changed their business model; and

▲ A healthy food company still in business after six years. I'm keeping my stock certificates in a drawer, holding my breath, hoping for an acquisition.

My career has flowed, and stopped, and started again, like an elaborate art project. A college student in a class I taught recently asked me how I made my career choices along the way. I told her didn't have a blueprint, but I paid attention to my inner voice, and I'm satisfied with the outcome, so far.

Though I'm not a serial entrepreneur, my business life looks like a series of startups because: I've followed my instincts, built relationships and partnerships, run lean, created my own opportunities, pivoted when I had to, and invested my time and (mostly) my own funds. The only missing creature in my life's "startup ecosystem" was a mentor. With one exception (which you can read about later) I've had to mentor myself.

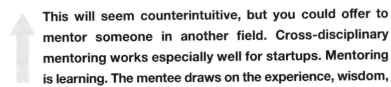

**This will seem counterintuitive, but you could offer to mentor someone in another field. Cross-disciplinary mentoring works especially well for startups. Mentoring is learning. The mentee draws on the experience, wisdom,**

> **and network of the mentor. The mentor explores new industries, learns new trends, and benefits from fresh thinking. Be both, at least once in your career. You might find a pathway to a new one.**

Today, in addition to my consulting practice, I'm a mentor for startup incubators and accelerators in Texas, California, and New York. Startup incubators take "infant" companies, ones that are at the idea stage, and help them get traction so they can apply to an accelerator, if they choose to. Accelerators offer more mature startup companies a little investment, guidance, and mentorship, a boot camp approach that can include intensive classes and workshops that prepare them for investment. Most accelerators take equity in the companies they help.

Once a month I hold office hours as a mentor for The Capital Factory in Austin. It's considered the center of the tech startup universe in Texas, with offices in Dallas and Houston. Capital Factory invests in dozens of companies a year here in Texas, and occasionally outside of the state.

I also mentor startups for Expert DOJO, an international early-stage accelerator based in Los Angeles. The founder, Brian McMahon (who kindly wrote the Foreword for this book), is a wise and witty Irishman with a keen eye for promising startups around the world. The DOJO has helped grow companies like StarNews in Africa, UNLU in India, and Sensate in the U.K. Plus Champions Round, Xicama, Potli cannabis edibles, and Woodpecker, a legal documents platform, among many other rising stars in the startup firmament.

For SKU, the first US startup accelerator for consumer products, I've advised the founders of food, hair care, and wellness companies. The SKU experience is different: We mentor as a team, each bringing in our own areas of expertise to help accelerate the startup's growth.

Whether you planned it or not, you may end up in a startup, too. COVID-19 forced a lot of us to consider reinventing ourselves. Even before the pandemic rocked our world, the "new world of work" was arriving faster than our education system could keep up. Automation, AI, and visionaries like Elon Musk are creating new career opportunities, while making old, familiar careers obsolete or at risk.

And if you consider yourself a creative and you don't think business is really your thing, startups might be a surprisingly good fit. They are commercial enterprises and they're meant to make money, but working with them scratches that itch that creatives are blessed with: We just want to create new products, new services, new ways to work, live, and thrive.

Starting up and starting over again and again has expanded my startup repertoire. I've been hired for strategic advice on product design and innovation, user experience, marketing and go-to-market strategies, business development and partnerships, and preparation for investment. Working in so many different fields and with such a wide variety of companies has also helped me build a useful and diverse network of experts and investors.

I'm so lucky, I feel like I'm riding a gravy train with biscuit wheels, as they say in the Lone Star State. I get to spend my time feasting at the buffet of new ideas. Chasing lots of shiny objects (feeding my ADD, a starting up superpower). Reading widely. Connecting people with opportunities. Helping others fulfill their dreams and bring their ideas to market and eventually, to investors.

Since March 2020 when the world stopped spinning, I've worked closely as a mentor or consultant to companies in skin care for people of color, content creation for small businesses, a biodegradable hand soap pod, two cannabis recruiting companies, a platform that helps foreign students find study opportunities abroad, an app to spread kindness and send messages of gratitude to essential workers, a rugged 3-D printer for the military, a marketplace matching Latin American developers with tech projects, a psilocybin research company, and a livestream shopping platform that bills itself as a QVC for the space age.

**What will people say? You can't control that. Some may be supportive. But don't expect other people to buy into your idea of starting over or starting a new company. Make your own choices. You're getting ready to get ready. And that's a good start.**

Repeatedly revving and stalling my career over many decades prepared me for the pandemic in ways I couldn't have imagined. It made me nimble and unflappable. I'm cautious but always optimistic. Like most seasoned entrepreneurs, I've learned to scan the horizon for threats and opportunities, and I can put my head down and work quickly and efficiently when that's what's required. In this book you'll see how I do it.

Whether you're a parent or not, single or not, young or close to retirement, it might be time to live like a startup, or to start a startup. Though this book is a memoir about me (hey, write your own book!) I've included lots of actionable tips for you, based on my successes and failures.

My personal roadmap into startups looks like one of·those

tours to celebrity homes in LA: lots of hills, curves, fences, and big gates to keep most people out. I've managed to climb those hills, take those curves, and jump over those fancy fences when I've needed to.

I'm from a rural, tobacco farming area. I went to a public university. I had no wealth, connections, or influence. I'm just an ordinary person, who's had some extraordinary opportunities, some of which came easily. Others, not so much.

Startup companies, campaigns, films, projects, books, and relationships all begin with a series of questions: What if? What if I could solve this problem? What if I don't start? What if I fail? What if I succeed? The only way to answer these questions is to make one small move in a new direction. See how it feels.

Successful fresh starts are built on the scaffolding of past decisions: Were you productive? Trustworthy? Agreeable? Honorable? If not, maybe it's time to look in the mirror. Clean up your mess. Then make your move, and going forward, follow the wise advice of "Soul Rocker" Michael Franti, who titled his 2020 pandemic album *Work Hard & Be Nice*.

Amen.

# Chapter 1
## Building Boats

I am not a Boomer.

I was born in the middle of the last century, but not everyone my age is a dinosaur. I've learned to keep my business tools sharpened and my mind open. I have to. I work with people who are young enough to be my grandchildren.

No matter how old you are, if you're feeling "stuck" in an unfulfilling job, maybe you've boxed yourself in by not challenging yourself. Or maybe you haven't allowed yourself to imagine all the possibilities outside your current field. This book will show you how someone who started with no connections, in some cases no experience, and no inheritance on the horizon, managed to build an exciting, successful life and career by continually starting up and starting over. So can you.

Maybe you're currently stuck in a dead-end job because you feel you have no choice. First, you always have a choice, but you may not want to risk your paycheck. If that's you, then use this book as an armchair traveler would read a guidebook to a foreign country: You may not be ready for your trip yet, but you can get the lay of the land for when you are.

Sometimes you may be starting up, sometimes starting over. Starting up can mean anything from a new job to a new relationship to a startup company. Starting over is a comeback, a do over.

As humans, no matter where we live or what language we speak, we yearn for a healthy mix of adventure and safety. We want to feed our families and take vacations. Sometimes we don't want to have to make choices but recognize that we must. Most important, we don't want to reach the end of our lives regretting the chances we didn't take, the opportunities we shouldn't have left behind.

No employer I ever met was looking for someone with my résumé. I wasn't a "this" or a "that" as a profession. I fell into most jobs by accident or through personal referrals from friends and colleagues. With a wide range of interests and a willingness to pay my dues in every decade of my work life, I've picked up a variety of useful skills and have been employable and employed most of the time. David Epstein's book *Range: Why Generalists Triumph in a Specialized World* validates my experience. Being a generalist is my specialty, and I'm grateful to draw on it as a startup skillset.

People with my kind of operating system have spent our lives compensating for the fact that we are mostly misfits in the world of org charts and job titles. Our inquiring minds can make us fascinating conversationalists, insightful strategists, useful travel companions: We always find the best restaurants because we've read all the reviews and asked the right people.

All I've ever done is take chances. I've rarely made the "safe" choice in my career. Yet I'm still standing. An inquisitive, avid reader and lifelong learner, my rapacious curiosity has impelled me to reinvent myself over and over. And that has made me fearless.

Have you ever used Ben Franklin's methods for making a decision such as "Do I stay or do I go?" He suggested to a friend (who was considering leaving his wife) that he fold a sheet of paper and write the pros on one side, cons on the other.

If you're a visual thinker, using the Ben Franklin method can help you clarify your thoughts. Since not all pros or cons are equally important, highlight the ones that are. This method strips these "tree of life" decisions down to the bare branches, so you can clearly see which limb will hold you, and which is more likely to let you fall.

I've been a wanderer, an artist, an inventor, and an entrepreneur, with all the attendant ups and downs in income and stability, changes of zip codes, and, too often, the terrifying feeling actors get after a movie wraps: "I'll never work again!"

In an unfriendly economy, it can be dangerous to leap without a net. Who would be crazy enough to leave a job to travel, take years away from business to be a stay-at-home mom, and start a new enterprise with a rebellious teenager at home? Me. It's been a thrill ride, and so far, it's been great. But first, the backstory. It's not chronological; that would make it too tempting to skip to the end. The juicy bits are peppered throughout, so stay with me.

My parents encouraged me to earn my own spending money, which I've done since I was 10 years old. For three summers I sold flower seeds door-to-door, earning cash and prizes. At 12, I started babysitting on the weekends, and ran a summer camp for pre-schoolers, called "Kiddie College." At 13, I had my first full-time summer job. I've found something interesting and satisfying about every job I've ever had, even the ones that were entry-level or where I was seriously underpaid. Then there were the "glamour" jobs I loved, with good pay, and great perks.

But it wasn't all bluebonnets and banjos in these jobs. Sometimes it was hell.

In 1981, in my 20s, I was a talent coordinator for the *Tomorrow* show at NBC when Roger Ailes, the man who went on to create Fox News, was hired as the executive producer. He changed the name to *Tomorrow Coast to Coast* and added a studio audience. The new shows included women in bikinis and furs, segments on sex with author Nancy Friday, and debates with antagonists like Reverend Jerry Falwell and sex magazine publisher Bob Guccione. That last one was my booking.

One day Roger called me into his office to tell me that I was capable of real brilliance, so I thought he was going to give me a raise. Then he lit into me, telling me he hated my background notes for that day's show. He threw them across the room at me.

Roger terrified me with his bombast and his scalding criticism. Despite his Santa belly, goatee, and droll sense of humor, he seemed to enjoy bullying people. Some nights I slept on the floor in my office. I had to be hospitalized because the stress of working for him had blocked my bladder: I couldn't pee for three days. I was afraid Roger was going to fire me for not working hard enough or long enough, and I wasn't the only one he terrorized. On the same day he had called me into his office he had a ferocious tantrum in a booking meeting with five other producers and this time he threw a briefcase across the room.

OK, maybe he was having a bad day. Still, inexcusable.

It never occurred to me to take my concerns about his behavior to HR. I was young, but I knew he had all the power. (Later in his life Roger's career would be derailed over charges of sexual harassment at Fox.)

ait for the boss to tell you you're falling short. r your own performance and ask for guidance upport from the friendlies among your peers. If keeping the job is the priority, starting over means improving your work product so you can keep the boss happy. Don't be shy about asking for help.

In the end, I learned a lot from Roger. He was a brilliant television programmer who deeply understood what TV audiences wanted, and he was a master at assuming and wielding power in a corporate setting. My job performance eventually exceeded his expectations. By the time the show was cancelled I felt I could call him anytime for a reference, though I never did.

Sometimes your horrible bosses, like your enemies, are your best teachers. Which of your employers or past clients were the most challenging to work for? What did you learn from that experience?

I have worked in and out of big companies and small ones, launched startups, and hired, fired, and mentored people. After 40+ years in the world of work it's difficult, if not impossible, to put me in a box and say, "this is what she does." I'm like a Pez dispenser handing out bits of wisdom and strategic advice. A genie. Gutsy enough to cold-call the White House and end up with a mind-blowing invitation. Humble enough to recognize my time at center stage has passed, even though I'm not done.

That's how I ended up in startups.

You're only done when you say you are, not before. Are you taking care of your physical and mental health?

**Starting up or starting over takes mental focus and physical stamina. Get your body and mind ready. Age, income, education, geography, cannot limit you—unless you let them.**

My family of origin is a microcosm of what used to be the middle class. Each of us has our own interests and education levels, aptitudes, and attitudes toward our careers. While I've worked in many roles and industries, my siblings, with a couple of exceptions, have remained in one line of work for most of their lives.

I have three brothers and five stepbrothers. Two have retired, two work in state government, two work for universities, one is a tech consultant, and one runs fishing charters in the Florida Keys. The boats they've all built for themselves and their families are safe and seaworthy.

We all build our own boats. Some leak. Some never leave the safety of the harbor. What kind of boat have you built?

**Give yourself the gift of a rainy day fund. And invest, invest, invest. In yourself, and in others. Even if you have to take small steps like starting with an online course or a micro-investment through an app or in a startup, do it.**

For some people, starting over means taking less risk, not starting a company.

**Have you considered working in government? Federal, state and local jobs involve some bureaucracy, for sure, but they make up for it by offering more job security, plus benefits.**

Your boat doesn't have to be big, or fancy, or powerful. It just has to keep you safe and above the water.

# Chapter 2
## Talking, Texas, and an AK 47

Southerners can't help ourselves when it comes to storytelling—plain facts are so unsatisfying. We need adjectives, metaphors, gestures—big drama.

When I was growing up in the 1960s the tut-tutting about marriages falling apart, teenagers acting up, and other town gossip was always conveyed in delicious, excruciating detail. A tumor could never be described without comparing it to an item in the produce aisle in the grocery store.

"Lord, yes, it was the size of a lemon/grapefruit/cantaloupe. It was *this* big!"

Ever since I learned to talk, I've talked to strangers. My dad observed my communication skills and saw the potential for me to expand my audience.

When I turned 13, he pulled out his well-worn Berlitz conversation book and began to teach me Spanish. I learned *"La pluma está sobre la mesa"*—the pen is on the table—and many other phrases during that summer of love in the 60s. I welcomed the opportunity to learn another language, first to communicate with the handsome South American exchange student boarding next door (I would later spend a few months with his family in Paraguay), and later as a marketable skill.

Even my teenage brain recognized that this would open a world of possibilities. All I had to do was what came most naturally to me: talk, talk, talk. More languages, more opportunities.

I was hooked on Spanish. Endless hours of listening to Vicki Carr singing "Grande, Grande, Grande" and other ballads pulled an emotional ripcord in me. I worked on improving my accent. My love for all things Latin American, especially music was, and still is, immutable.

As I became a better singer and speaker, it built my confidence and self-esteem. In college, I prepared myself for a career that would somehow leverage my language ability.

**Consider downloading the language app Duolingo or buying a program like Rosetta Stone. Being a fluent Spanish speaker helped me get news assignments in Central America, producing jobs for St. Jude Children's Hospital and Beachbody, and an opportunity to sing professionally. Who knows where a new language skill could take you?**

Knowing another language not only makes you more valuable in the workplace, it opens your mind to other ways of thinking. You'll find plenty of books and articles about how language colors perceptions, and how through language study you can deepen your understanding of another culture. Studying other languages—French, Sanskrit, Ukrainian, and now Mandarin—has enriched my life and broadened my horizons.

University of Texas at Austin, early 1970s. I declared my major—Romance Languages—during freshman orientation, and never wavered. Moving from my little village to Austin was a radical shift: There were two thousand more people in my freshman dorm than in my entire hometown.

If I wanted company, all I had to do was scan the crowd for a friendly face, sit down, and start talking. This was a revelation and a welcome consolation for the relentlessly bullied kid with no friends before high school. We'll pick up this thread later in the book.

I surrounded myself with exchange students from Central and South America, making their fiestas the centerpiece of my social life. I set my sights on a career as a UN interpreter and translator.

To test this career choice, I decided to translate *El Tunel* by Ernesto Sabato, a short, but gripping psychological thriller. In those pre-Amazon days, I couldn't locate a copy in English for my dad, and I wanted to share the book with him. I spent four weeks trying to capture the action and adventure described in the original text, writing, erasing, and rewriting my translated paragraphs on yellow legal pads. I typed my finished translation and gave it to him for Father's Day. He loved it.

After that arduous task, though, I decided translating was not something I was meant to do. Too boring!

In college I studied Sanskrit, because I was told it was an "easy A" and took several optional courses on 16th and 17th century Spanish literature. I minored in Portuguese because I loved Brazilian music, and the Brazilian students had the best parties. Fluency in both languages has generated a lot of opportunities for me in more than one field—and with more than one boyfriend!

**Never underestimate the power of a business skill to improve your personal life.** The more arrows in your quiver (education, special skills, your network, persistence, patience) the more successful you will be in your career, and possibly, your love life.

After college, I was offered a generous short-term contract in the publications division of the Inter-American Development Bank in Washington, DC. They hired me to track the print production of the bank's annual report, as it was edited simultaneously in four languages. It was my first experience using a Gantt chart to manage a project.

At that early stage of my career, I discovered that project management was not my thing, even though I was pretty good at it. The Gantt chart helped me keep all the images, charts, and editorial content organized and on track for the term of my four-month contract.

Bullet dodged.

**You may stumble a few times as you find your footing early in your career, or whenever you start a new job. It's okay. You're learning.** If you're just starting out, or even if you're mid-career or later, follow the philosophy of the startup: Recognize that failure is a possibility. Just try your best to learn something from your mistakes.

In 1984, CBS News sent me to El Salvador with *Morning News* anchor Diane Sawyer. I had to set up interviews with the two presidential candidates: José Napoleón Duarte and Roberto D'Aubuisson. We traveled to San Salvador with Diane's then-boyfriend, Richard Holbrooke, who many years later became an ambassador, then assistant secretary of state in the Clinton administration. Walking through the airport with Diane was a revelation. All eyes were on her as she maneuvered through the crowds like a graceful gazelle. Richard and I were all but invisible.

I'd had previous experiences with Larry King's fans when I was his producer, and we took his radio show on the road. The network publicity machine had turned him into a minor celebrity, but women never responded to Larry the way men reacted to Diane. She was, and still is, stunning.

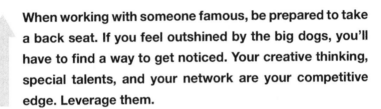

**When working with someone famous, be prepared to take a back seat. If you feel outshined by the big dogs, you'll have to find a way to get noticed. Your creative thinking, special talents, and your network are your competitive edge. Leverage them.**

On election eve in San Salvador, Diane and Richard were back at the hotel while I spent time getting to know "Blowtorch Bob" D'Aubuisson (named for his favorite interrogation tool) at his presidential campaign headquarters. After my pre-interview with this death-squad commander, one of the most notorious far-right leaders in Central American history, the crew was piling back into the van to leave.

It was almost midnight. We were all tired and ready to head back to the CBS bureau that was set up in our hotel. The previous night helicopters had kept the newbies among us on edge, sleeping with our curtains drawn to protect us from flying glass, moving into the bathtubs with our pillows when the noise became unbearable. Okay, I was the only newbie, and that's what I did.

There was no electricity within a three-block radius of the heavily fortified campaign headquarters because, according to our local fixers, the Duarte government didn't want D'Aubuisson receiving election results in real-time. There was no moon, and the only light came from headlights our driver had turned on in the van.

Because we were technically in a war zone, white duct tape with the letters "TV" covered part of our windshield, and our locally made tee shirts read "Periodista: No Dispare" (Journalist: Don't Shoot). Larry Doyle, a producer who had covered wars all over the world, was standing outside the van when I crossed the road.

A small sputtering car drove slowly, about eight feet away, nearly blocking our exit from the parking lot. A skinny young man in a black tee shirt rolled down the tinted passenger window, and we could see he wasn't alone. He pointed to me and shouted *"Oye, tenemos un mensaje para la prensa."* I barely had time to ask what their message was for the press when the window rolled down a little farther and the shouter pointed an AK 47 directly at my chest.

Larry, a legendary, heroic, award-winning producer for CBS was wearing a Kevlar vest, and he may not remember this, but he ducked, behind me! I hit the gravel and held my breath. Seconds felt like hours. All I heard was the squawk of the crew's radio when the bureau chief called, demanding to know why we weren't back at the hotel by curfew.

Then muffled laughter, screeching tires, and the car sped up the hill and out of sight. That's as close as I ever want to come to the barrel of a gun, and so far, no gun has come closer. War correspondents, I salute you. I'm no hero. As an associate producer for the *CBS Morning News*, my salary was respectable, but not enviable, certainly not enough to risk my life for this job. I knew then I wasn't cut out for hazardous, unpredictable assignments.

Like all scary moments in life, when you pump adrenaline, endorphins come along for the ride. I understand why some journalists are drawn to dangerous assignments: It's thrilling—but not for me.

Danger aside, working in network TV news is an adventure, the perfect arena for me because it meant learning about things, then telling other people about them. It requires a quick mind and an ability to take a deep dive into a variety of subjects—ideal for someone with ADD. Plus, in those days being a news producer at a TV network was a lot saner and more civilized than it is today, with 24-hour cable TV, live-streaming, and social media.

Not everyone aspires to be in front of the camera. That's where the big money is, certainly, but it's also where the stakes are highest and the competition fiercest. There's no margin for error since the words come out of your own mouth. Deciding to stay behind the camera at that point in my career may have limited my potential income, but it also gave me more job security, if I wanted it. Besides, it just seemed like a better fit.

Producers help shape news stories. A producer is like a mom: a multi-talented multitasker able to work on intense and frequent deadlines with all types of personalities and temperaments, toiling behind the scenes to make the people on camera look good. Correspondents on major news programs often step in after producers have laid the groundwork, done some of the interviews and, in some cases, put most of the story together, minus the on camera "standups." Yet the only face people recognize is the person in front of the camera.

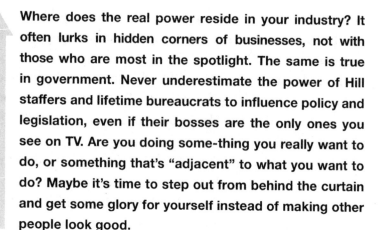

Where does the real power reside in your industry? It often lurks in hidden corners of businesses, not with those who are most in the spotlight. The same is true in government. Never underestimate the power of Hill staffers and lifetime bureaucrats to influence policy and legislation, even if their bosses are the only ones you see on TV. Are you doing some-thing you really want to do, or something that's "adjacent" to what you want to do? Maybe it's time to step out from behind the curtain and get some glory for yourself instead of making other people look good.

# Chapter 3
## Trouble with Politics

Speaking Spanish like a native helped me land my first paid job in politics. I was administrative assistant to a state representative with a district full of Spanish speakers. I had seen an ad for the position in the Daily Texan, the UT student newspaper, and decided to write a letter applying for the job in English, accompanied by a Spanish translation.

The legislature was only in session for a few months every two years (because Texans don't want their elected officials to do too much damage), but most staff stays employed year-round. Fortunately, my salary covered tuition and living expenses for my last two years of college. The job also fueled a lifelong interest in politics and current events.

In 1976, after I graduated from UT, the Jimmy Carter campaign asked me to volunteer to do some "door knocking" in the Spanish speaking areas of Houston. At the election night party in a private home, I ate a pot brownie. It was my first experience with cannabis. I was always too afraid to try it as a college student, but Carter's campaign people were doing it, so I thought "Why not?"

I didn't feel anything after the first brownie, so I ate another one. Still didn't feel anything, so I consumed two more. We were all watching the election returns on TV when I heard my friend Lynda in a sleepy (stoned) voice say, "Hey, Jeannie, Jimmy won." I said, "Great! I can't find my hands. Where are my hands? Where are my hands?"

I was sitting on them.

I stayed away from cannabis for many years after that night.

When Carter won, the campaign offered me a temp job on the White House transition team. I had worked to help "Jimmy" get elected, and I was thrilled to be on the path to what I hoped would be an exciting four years in the White House.

Do you want to start over in politics? Beware. It's an extremely competitive, unsavory, unfair business with a disproportionate share of toadies and those who lust for power at any price. Yet there are also some wonderful, thoughtful, righteous people, elected and unelected, who view politics as a public service. There's a reason why Washington and Hollywood love each other. They understand each other, deeply. Stars rise and fall, and those associated with them see their fortunes rise and fall with them.

**If politics is your calling, be prepared to hang onto someone's coattails until you make it. And hope that the candidate rewards your loyalty. No guarantees.**

My boss stuck me in a windowless room with stacks of boxes filled with résumés. Each one had a green line drawn across the top border, indicating the job candidate was in the Talent Inventory Program (TIP). TIP was an exclusive club of insiders, party officials, friends of the Carters, and constituents of powerful senators. You get the idea. I was instructed to make the first cut among these candidates for what they call "plum" government positions, or Schedule C jobs in the State Department, from assistant secretaries to ambassadors.

I only lasted a few weeks in that stuffy back room. I decided that even if I was offered a job in the West Wing, I didn't want it. I had no interest in working for a government run by yahoos who place inexperienced 20-somethings like me on the front lines of their job-placement operation, even though I deeply admired Jimmy Carter.

Some of the best career advice I've ever received came from a good friend at the mid-point of my career: "Always follow a lead where it takes you and always take everything to the point of offer."

 **You don't have to say yes to everything. You can turn down a job if you want to, but make it your choice, on your timetable, not theirs.**

# Chapter 4
# Low Salary, High Life: You Can Have Both

I've been flat broke, often. There was a time when I was one or two paychecks from homelessness, even when I worked on the White House transition team. My life path has been a spiral. I've learned and relearned lessons about finances and self-sufficiency on my way up the long, winding staircase of an eclectic career. Though it would take me years to get my financial footing, my first big break came when I got off the elevator on the wrong floor.

I was at an inflection point, three years out of college and about to get a job offer in broadcasting, just where I was meant to be. A passion I'd discovered in my lonely teen years would lead me to dinner on a movie set with a celebrity, a year of luxury living with an oil heiress, and a few dates with one of the astronauts who walked on the moon.

Here's how it happened.

Crystal City, Virginia, in the mid 1970s was a thick maze of high-rise buildings with no charm, no vibe, and no soul. The color palette ranged from creamy beige to muddy brown.

I had a plan to leverage my limited political experience and my language ability to wrangle a job in a think tank writing nerdy policy papers that would, perhaps, influence lawmakers on Capitol Hill. But I got lost looking for the think tank's offices.

Turns out I was in the right brown building, on the wrong floor. I saw a sign on the wall to the right of the elevator: Mutual Radio Network. I decided to take my chances. I stepped off the elevator and saw a vacant reception desk with a chair behind it. All four of the doors leading to the interior offices were locked, requiring a badge to enter.

I sat down at the desk.

As I waited in this windowless purgatory people would open one door, walk across the lobby, and close the other door behind them without acknowledging me. They all looked extremely busy, so I kept waiting patiently.

Would you have waited?

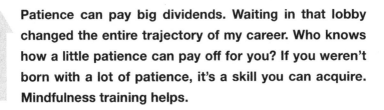

**Patience can pay big dividends. Waiting in that lobby changed the entire trajectory of my career. Who knows how a little patience can pay off for you? If you weren't born with a lot of patience, it's a skill you can acquire. Mindfulness training helps.**

Who knew that I had set the stage for this moment in childhood? In my early teens I was desperate for contact with the world outside the boundaries of my small community. I used to sneak my parents' portable radio out of the kitchen, place it under my pillow, and listen to the news and interviews on the Mutual Black Network, carried on WBBM in Chicago.

My mother never understood why it was so hard for me to get

up every morning for school. She had no idea I was as devoted to talk radio as I was to Latin music and that I stayed up most of the night, every night, furtively listening in on radio conversations. Like a little spy.

What did you do when you were young that could have predicted where you are today? Is there something you used to love that you've left behind? What's stopping you from pursuing it? Start with worst possible outcome. Is that likely to happen? Have you ever allowed yourself to imagine the best possible outcome? How do you know whether to pay attention to your fears or your dreams? Good question. Just trust, do your best, and be open to new challenges and opportunities, even those that happen by accident. Embrace the serendipity.

When I finally stood up to leave, cameras must have caught me, because one of the locked doors swung open and a woman asked what I wanted. I handed her my résumé. She read it and walked back through the door. After about 10 minutes she returned and took me back to the newsroom to meet the news director. By now I had worked in retail, politics, the InterAmerican Development Bank, and on the White House transition team. In some respects, I might have appeared overqualified for what they would ask me to do, though I most definitely was not.

"I'm going to make you the next Connie Chung," the news director said. "I put Connie Chung on the air, and I'll do the same for you. In the meantime, I need you to tear copy from the AP and Reuters news wire machines and give it to the reporters. Also, you'll have to collect their timesheets and help me with payroll." With stars in my eyes, I agreed to his lowball offer, and started work the next day.

> **Don't be afraid to negotiate.** As Herb Cohen, author of *You Can Negotiate Anything* said on the Larry King Show "If you think you've got power, you've got it, even if you don't have it. You have it." Salary, benefits, working remotely, vacation days, paid continuing education, parking, gym memberships, are just a few of the items you can ask for before you agree to start a new job, or take a new position in your company.

Two weeks into my new job my boss, the news director, was fired. I would miss him, but that's showbiz. His replacement was an affable, pipe-smoking, old-fashioned newsman with a deep baritone voice and a soft spot for someone new to the business. I knew nothing about journalism, radio, unions, Washington, nada. I learned on the job.

After my one-year anniversary, the network signed Larry King and moved his local radio show from Miami to our headquarters in Crystal City. Larry wanted to replace his producer, and my boss said if I finished all my other work, I could book guests for Larry's show. I got a raise from $200 to $210 a week. (It was 1978 and this was nearly twice the federal minimum wage, but it wasn't easy to pay rent on that salary.)

> **A low-paying job can give you a chance to learn a new industry and build your network. Consider it paid vocational training. And keep the contact info for everyone you meet. You never know when you might be able to help each other.**

Booking guests was new to me, but my conversational skills helped me develop confidence and competence. I put together a persuasive pitch, built an extensive list of contacts, and sweet-talked them ten words a minute, with gusts of fifty, as my fellow Texans might observe. I convinced prominent people that Larry was the next big thing in network radio, and they simply must do his show. Usually it worked.

Larry King was a nobody in Washington when he first started on the network. I had to persuade our high-profile, talk-show guests to take a taxi to our studios late at night, pay for it themselves, and make sure they could find our building in the dark (no Google maps in those days). They had to take one elevator down to the basement, get off, then switch to another one to get up to the 12th floor. Sometimes they made it through this gauntlet and ended up in our elevator lobby, banging on the door. Other times they ended up stuck in the basement. In those days before cellphones, a few guests, including members of Congress, found themselves trapped until I went down to look for them when it was close to airtime. One Washington official complained to the network about this inconvenience, but the president of the network told him to get lost. The network wouldn't even pay cab fares. They weren't about to pay for a security guard/escort.

A few months later my boss officially gave me the job and the title: Producer, *The Larry King Show*, plus another $15 a week. That's $11,700 a year to produce a national radio show.

I didn't care. I was thrilled. Naïve but thrilled.

*The Larry King Show* aired live five nights a week from midnight to 5:30 a.m. I don't know how Larry survived all those years of that nightly slog. My schedule was brutal, too. I'd come into the office at 11:00 p.m., start the show at midnight, get home by 6:00 a.m., unplug my phone, sleep until 2:00 p.m., then book guests for the next few days, which sometimes took all afternoon. This was my life five days a week.

I lived in a $500 a month apartment over a garage that had a pitched roof so steep I had to lean my head back in the kitchen to do the dishes. There were no closets, so I had a dress rack on wheels and hung my underwear from the ceiling in wire produce baskets. Good thing I was single and didn't eat much. The refrigerator was Lilliputian.

Once, on a rare night off, I decided to invite a Larry King guest to my apartment after we had gone out on a date. It was Harrison Schmidt, at the time a US senator from New Mexico. He had walked on the moon as a member of the crew of Apollo 17. Imagine what a US Senator/astronaut must have thought of that apartment. Actually, it was probably familiar to him, not much bigger than his space capsule! Nothing untoward happened on that date, but I did ask him to take his shoes off so I could say I touched the feet that touched the moon. He indulged me. I'll never forget it. What a guy!

Working for *The Larry King Show* was a fever dream for a devoted talk radio fan. Larry had no peer as a raconteur, and the stories he told when we were off the air were priceless. I'm sure some of them were true.

He once told me a story about leaving the record on at his radio station in Miami while he left to meet a listener-temptress for a tryst. This superfan had the radio tuned to his station as they were making out, and she heard the needle skipping over and over again on the Harry Belafonte record he'd left on in his DJ booth. He claims he ran back to the station to remedy the situation, but he was locked out. Truth? Or tall tale? I'll never know.

In those days Larry didn't sleep much, spending many of his mornings at the track, betting on the ponies. He always needed money, and he used to borrow a few dollars from me for coffee and donuts, but I didn't care. I was doing what I loved, working for someone who made my life bigger and more exciting than I'd ever imagined.

I finally got a raise to $250 a week.

We took the show on the road a few weeks every year, stayed in five-star hotels, rode in limos, and ate in great restaurants. But I'd come home to an empty refrigerator and not enough in my bank account to pay the rent. One month I had to sell my car to pay my landlord. I was too proud to ask anyone for help. Fortunately, my finances improved significantly when I finally decided to make a move.

**If you're looking to make a change in your life but you're thinking of all the reasons why you can't, don't throw yourself a pity party. Identify someone who could be your future mentor, business partner or employer. Look on LinkedIn, buy industry magazines, ask around. Find someone who is already doing what you'd like to do. Connect with her (or him) and ask for advice and/or introductions. Wear a smile. You know how you take selfies showing your good side? Everyone has strengths. Emphasize yours.**

One day I got a call from a gentleman who said he'd heard Larry say on the air that I might be getting serious with someone, and he wanted to meet me before I made a lifetime commitment to anyone else. He was both an architect and an MD, and in those pre-Internet days I had to do real research, with the help of a reference librarian. His background checked out, so I agreed to a date.

When I opened the door to my apartment, I did a double take. He looked like Vegas legend Vic Damone: gold chains, leisure suit, and poufy dyed black hair. Against my better judgment, I grabbed my coat and got in his car. We had dinner at a nice, intimate restaurant on the Potomac river where we shared a bottle of expensive wine. Then we went back to his house where we sat in his comfortable library and sipped French brandy.

What he did next stunned me. He unfurled the blueprints for his new house, complete with a baby's room that he expected me to fill. It was the creepiest first date I had ever had, for sure. I was still in my early 20s and my executive function wasn't optimized for these kinds of situations. Plus, I had had wine and brandy. Good thing he was a gentleman. Or maybe he was afraid I'd tell Larry. I gently told him that Larry was making up stories, and I just wasn't ready to settle down. He drove me home, and I never heard from him again.

**Has your boss (or a co-worker) tried to set you up on a date? What would that do to your career if the date didn't work out? Awkward. Are you in a relationship with a co-worker or boss? Uh oh. Proceed with caution.**

One of our late-night guests, Donald Sutherland, invited me to the set of a movie he was filming in DC, *Nothing Personal*, co-starring Suzanne Somers. Probably the worst movie he ever made, and he knew it, but like many actors, even famous ones, he hated to turn down work. We had dinner in his trailer, with his assistant. I was thrilled to be on a movie set with an actor I'd seen many times on the big screen. He knew how to give a small-town girl a thrill letting me have a taste of Hollywood. I was starstruck. The perks of this job were undeniable, despite my meager paycheck.

Elinor DeVore, an oil heiress who had written a book of poetry to raise money for breast cancer, was a frequent guest on *The Larry King Show*. She invited me to her apartment in the Watergate and asked me to help her write her memoir. Her former husband had insured movie productions, and she had spent weeks with Elizabeth Taylor and Richard Burton on the set of *Cleopatra*, among other grand adventures. She said she wanted to share her stories with the world, but I think that was only partly true. Ellie was wealthy, astute, single, kind-hearted, and lonely. She wanted a confidante, a playmate. And I wanted an Auntie Mame.

We spent our afternoons drinking Vouvray from her Baccarat glasses and eating beluga caviar delivered from Jean-Louis, the posh restaurant downstairs. We also spent a few hours a day working on the book, which we never completed. We were having too much fun.

My days were getting busier, but booking guests was easier as Larry raised his profile in Washington power circles. Finally, PR people and congressional staffers were calling me to get their people booked on the show. Our audience grew from 30 to 300 stations my first year as producer. My birthplace was only a few hours away, but my "big" job and those afternoons on Ellie's balcony at the Watergate transformed me: My past was a foreign country I never wanted to visit again. I was growing into this lifestyle, and I wasn't going back.

Though I lived a glamorous life with Ellie, my own finances were still a wreck. Ellie let me wear her jewelry and her St. Laurent clothes and shoes, but it all felt like make-believe. I kind of wanted her to adopt me.

> **Childhood poverty is not destiny. Designer clothes, caviar, and limousines are all fun perks of wealth, and one day they may come your way, even temporarily. But they're not important. If you were alive in 2020, you've learned what matters most. Friends, family, good health.**

My parents kept telling me to look for a job that paid more, but it took me a long time to follow their advice. Anyone who's been in the media knows how addicting it can be. It really is as exciting and entertaining as everyone thinks it is, and you do meet interesting people. You're surrounded by the extremes of society: the notorious, the scandalous, the powerful and the well-to-do, even if you aren't one of them. But a couple of hundred dollars a week wasn't even enough to buy gas for my daily trips to the Watergate, after I'd paid my bills. I clearly needed a bigger salary.

It turns out I'd laid the stepping-stones to my next career move without realizing it at the time. During my last year with Larry King, I had scanned the credits on a late-night TV show on NBC, *Tomorrow* with Tom Snyder. I periodically sent booking suggestions to a senior producer there, Bob Carman. He was close to retirement, which may be why he was much more approachable than most network producers would have been. We struck up a friendship on the phone, and I nurtured this connection for almost a year, simply because I was a fan of his show. Then, I really needed to call in a favor.

> **Focusing on the horizon helps with seasickness because with stable visual information, you adjust your "body sway." You may feel unmoored as you contemplate starting up or starting over. Try to look at your destination through wide lens, placing all the future scenarios, good and bad, in your field of vision. Change can be terrifying, and it can also lead to a better life. Focusing on the best possible outcomes as you consider the possible negatives will help you stay balanced.**

After two years as Larry's producer, I was still making $250 a week. I would start over if I had to, but not until I tried to negotiate a better deal with the Mutual Broadcasting System. I went to the president of the network and demanded a real salary. He feigned sympathy. Then he reached into his prize closet (broadcasters often have a closet filled with products they advertise) and he offered me a 15-pound dry-cured Virginia ham instead.

"Merry Christmas," he said.

> **Keep your eyes open. You'll know when it's time to move on and start over. If you're mid-career, don't let your ego or your identification with your job title or company get in the way.**

I quit the same day I got the ham. I rode the DC Metro with that ham for hours, wondering if I had made a terrible mistake.

I pondered my next move. Larry had left messages on my home phone all afternoon, but I was just riding the rails, thinking. Holding onto that ham. That ham represented how little I was valued by my employer, and I was pissed.

When I finally spoke to Larry that evening, I told him, "It's not me. It's not you. It's the ham. I just can't do it anymore."

After all my Metro ponderings I had come to realize the network was trying to get me to quit so they wouldn't have to pay unemployment. Mutual was the world's cheapest employer, no doubt about it.

The day I quit, Jack Kirby, who would later become one of my closest friends, and a mentor, was in the building. Jack had been a local radio producer in Boston and Philadelphia. Although he denies it, I'm sure all those boys, including Larry, were plotting to have Jack replace me all along.

Quitting without giving notice is never a good idea. It's not wise to burn bridges. But sometimes you have to reclaim your dignity, especially when you feel you're being exploited. Fortunately, it's easy to replace one low-paying job with another that pays the same, or even more.

**Have you decided you've had enough? Have you thought about what you'll need for a soft landing? You can negotiate. Ask for a recommendation letter, more severance, or other benefits. Don't burn the house down when you leave. Employers sometimes take it personally when you leave on your timetable, not theirs. Let them down gently.**

49

# Chapter 5
# No Experience? No Problem!

Bob Carman, NBC *Tomorrow* show producer:
"Have you ever worked in television?"

Me: "No."

Bob: "What makes you think you can do it? You've only been in radio."

Me: "Everything I've ever done is something I've never done before."

Bob: "You're not afraid?"

Me: "Never."

And that is exactly how I made the giant leap from radio to TV. Bob took a chance on me. He had "aged out" of being a producer for *The Tonight Show with Johnny Carson* and had landed at what would be his last job in TV, at *Tomorrow*. He believed in me, and when I needed him to go to bat for me, he came through.

 **Comedian Jonathan Winters said "If your ship doesn't come in, swim out to meet it." The more you build and nurture your network, the greater your chances of**

**getting a referral or a tip about a new opportunity. If you are introverted, it's OK. In the age of the Internet, you don't have to meet people in person, so long as your phone, email and messaging game is on point.**

I never imagined I'd live in New York City. Growing up, I'd longed to travel and live in faraway places, but New York was not on my wish list. Ever. One summer, when I was in elementary school, my family bypassed the city on the way to spend a week with my cousins at their summer home on Fire Island. Looking out the rear window of our station wagon as we crossed the Verazzano-Narrows Bridge toward Long Island, Manhattan appeared dingy, gloomy, menacing.

While I was waiting for Bob Carman's boss to agree to interview me for the NBC job, I took a short-term position at the World Bank. I was administrative assistant to a Swiss mediator tasked with closing the East African Development Bank. My boss had to negotiate a fair way to divide the assets among the member countries. He traveled back and forth from Nairobi to Dodoma to Kampala, where he had to negotiate with the "Butcher of Uganda," Idi Amin. Dr. Victor Umbricht had a dangerous assignment, one that could involve his own kidnapping, murder, or at the least, hurt his reputation if he didn't get the job done.

This position gave me a front row seat for some high stakes diplomacy, and I learned a lot from him in a very short time. My boss was brilliant, a courteous older gentleman, but there was no way I would have stayed in that bureaucracy after my three-month contract was up, even if I didn't have another job (fingers crossed) in the queue. I was shocked by the extravagant spending and lack of accountability in that bloated international organization in those days. I held out hope that the NBC job would come through.

Pamela Burke, the *Tomorrow* executive producer, finally agreed to interview me, and she hired me as a talent coordinator. She said I would be on probation for six weeks, though, an easy way out if Tom Snyder didn't like me. I sold my furniture, gave away most of my clothes, and made the move to the Big Apple, with some reservations about living in the city I'd been afraid of when I was younger. I didn't doubt I would easily make the transition to TV. I had booked guests for Larry King: I knew what to do.

At the end of the fifth week there I asked Pam if I could stay.

Pam: "What do you mean by 'stay'?"

Me; "Well, you hired me conditionally for six weeks. It's been five weeks already."

Pam: "Of course you're staying. Why would you not stay?"

Me: "Yes, I want to stay."

Pam: "OK."

Me: "OK."

That's how I went from "probationary" to "permanent" employee at NBC.

**Is there something you'd like to ask the boss about but you're afraid of what the answer might be? Feedback on your performance maybe? It's possible the answer isn't what you're anticipating. Maybe it's better.**

I had rolled the dice on a big career change once before, when I applied to Braniff, the airline that competed with Pan Am on routes to South America. I wanted to be a flight attendant, and I was sure my fluency in Spanish would give me an edge. After my second round of interviews in Dallas, I was so convinced I would get the job, I sold everything I owned back then (which was very little, no furniture) and waited for the offer letter.

**Trust and acceptance provide the forward thrust you'll need to start something new. Trust opens the throttle to transformation, and acceptance is each breath you take on the way through to the other side. How do you decide whom to trust? How many obstacles are you are willing to go around or over? Don't start anything new before you answer these questions. #fortunecookiewisdom**

While I was waiting for my offer letter, I flew Braniff on a domestic flight and had to translate for a woman sitting next to me who was a nervous flier. The flight attendants on that plane didn't speak Spanish as well as I did, and I told myself this airline would be crazy not to hire me, but a few weeks later I learned I didn't make the final cut. I was shattered, but not for long.

I had an epiphany.

I finally understood that I was not the one in charge of this whole career thing. No matter how much I wanted something, or believed I was a perfect fit, life/the universe/spirit/fate/God had other plans for me. I had taken a leap of faith again, this time assuming I'd wow NBC. I was in my mid-20s, in 1980, with a high-profile network radio job on my résumé, and I was confident they would hire me. I didn't want to be famous. I just wanted to work in network TV. And I did it.

Take that, small-town bullies.

Dateline: somewhere in the South, late 1950s. I wasn't allowed to start first grade with my peer group because the cutoff for entering school was September 30, before my sixth birthday. I had been reading since I was a toddler, so my mom decided to homeschool me for a while.

When the principal allowed me to bypass first grade a few months later, the bullying began. First of all, I was the best reader in the class; second, I had a face full of freckles. And at the teacher's request, I would often Show and Tell my classmates about my grandparents' world travels. Strike three.

I was gullible, sensitive, and desperate to be liked. The mean boys at school recognized my weaknesses and probably knew I would never fight back. They invented a nasty game and often played it in the cafeteria in front of all the other students. One of them would touch me, then run to the others and spread "Jeannie germs." If a boy had his fingers crossed, he was considered "safe."

This was not harmless, as anyone who has been bullied can confirm. But there was only one school in this town. I was forced to suck it up, all the way to seventh grade. The sting of unpopularity marked me then, and it will never be completely gone. It's an uncomfortable part of my history, but as I've moved on it's made me deeply empathetic toward people who are marginalized or abused.

A loving family is not enough to inoculate a child from the acute, blistering pain and persistent insecurity bullies emboss on a young person's soul. Some kids get trapped in a victim's mindset and never outgrow it. Others, like me, become people-pleasers.

 **Are you a bully? Check yourself. Stop it. Have you been bullied? Don't let it consume your life. You don't have to put up with it. Confront the bully or enlist some help.**

As a female raised in the South, it felt natural to wear the mask of a people-pleaser. Not helpful in a male-dominated world. That BS finally stopped when my periods ended at menopause. Something to look forward to, ladies.

Menopause made me the ninja I am today. But ladies, you don't have to wait until menopause to check in with yourself and reinvent. And gentlemen, consider it reparations for all those years of horrible cramps and PMS. Count your blessings.

A few weeks before I was scheduled to start my NBC job at 30 Rockefeller Plaza (30 Rock), my heiress friend Ellie moved to New York. She'd bought a co-op on the Upper East Side, and offered me a beautiful, lavishly furnished guest bedroom. I hadn't found an apartment yet, so how could I say no?

Ellie continued to spoil me, and I basked in her attention. She was charming and she reminded me of my mother with her unquenchable thirst for new experiences. She had a beautiful, fully equipped kitchen but we never cooked at home. We had expensive restaurant takeout or went out for dinner almost every night. I slept well on her luxurious imported sheets, wore her beautiful couture clothes (again), and networked at her parties with her fancy friends. In spite of our 20-year age difference, we had a lot of fun together. She took me shopping with her almost every week, hiring a car and driver to wait for us as we ran in and out of the stores on Madison Avenue.

Sign of the Dove was one of our favorite restaurants. One evening at dinner there, Ellie got into a conversation with a charming older man at the next table. He invited us back to his townhouse. Leonard Stern, the founder of the Hartz Mountain bird food company, was a recently divorced billionaire, and you could have parked a semi full of parakeets in his gargantuan fireplace. It was the grandest private home I'd ever seen. Too bad he was too old for both of us. He was gracious and charming.

A year later, on a pre-interview for *Tomorrow Coast to Coast*, I would visit another sensational townhouse nearby, this one belonging to the publisher of *Penthouse*. Bob Guccione and his girlfriend had so much gold furniture I practically needed sunglasses inside.

Since those early days living it up in Washington, DC, and Manhattan, I've stayed in a number of nice homes around the world, but the little country girl never left me. I can still remember knocking on the neighbor's door, trying to sell her the lettuce from our refrigerator after my parents had an argument over the grocery bills. A young entrepreneur, I saw a problem and tried to solve it.

These days I'm not as impressed as I used to be by the perks of hanging around the rich and famous. If you follow entertainment news you've seen that their lives are not always enviable. The Notorious B.I.G.rapped about "Mo money, mo problems." It's true. The rich and famous just have more stuff. More places to put it. More people to take care of it for them. And often, more problems.

A few months after I'd moved in with Ellie, her old lover, a white-collar criminal, was released from prison. I know. Whoa! She'd never mentioned him to me before.

He wanted to move in with her, and he didn't want any roommates. Ellie helped me find a tiny studio apartment a few blocks away for $900 a month. I was making $5,000 a month by then, so this was very affordable. I bought a Murphy bed, some high thread-count sheets, and settled in.

I started dating a movie-star-handsome secret service agent I'd met backstage at NBC. The other agents called him Clint because whenever he would advance a trip for a member of the First Family, invariably the women he met would swoon over him as if he were a younger Clint Eastwood. And that's about all I can say about that relationship.

Sorry. Secret.

Sometimes I've felt so capable in a job I went on autopilot. But whenever a new boss arrived, I would have to snap out of it and figure out how to respond to whatever incoming he (almost always it was a "he") decided to aim my way.

Pam, my first boss at NBC, was let go only a few months after she'd hired me. When the network replaced her with the notorious Roger Ailes, he came in spraying the territory like a dog. He told me he'd once put his fist through the wall of a control room "to show the talent who's boss." He was a hemophiliac, so this was not advised, but control room walls are usually padded particleboard, so he probably didn't get hurt. And by telling this story he proved his point. He wasn't going to let Tom, "the talent," push him around.

*Tomorrow* had been moved from the network's news division to the entertainment division and expanded from an hour to ninety minutes. Roger wanted to make some major changes to reflect the new mandate of the show: no more intimate conversations with Tom smoking on the set. Now it was Wendy Williams and the Plasmatics blowing up TV sets during their performance, Elvis Costello, and, for Thanksgiving, the world champion turkey caller—my booking.

Roger wasn't happy with the team of booker/producers he had inherited, including me, as I recounted earlier. He recruited West Coast TV hot shot Shelley Ross, who went on to become executive producer of *Good Morning America* and *CBS Morning News*. He also hired Andrea Ambandos, who years later built a business that made her, in her words, the "Fellini of Fitness." She's the founder of Dragonfly Productions and the creative force behind some of the most wildly successful infomercials and home workout videos, as well as fitness streaming services for NBC, Beachbody, and others.

At first, I was intimidated by these two formidable women, but we were in the foxhole together and soon became close friends and supportive co-workers.

*Sex and the City* could have been written about us, minus the Manolos.

Okay, Shelley had Manolos. And I had a Secret Service boyfriend we nicknamed Secret Lovees. The three of us were young, frisky, and unstoppable.

With our influential positions in network TV, we had free tickets to Broadway shows and invitations to parties at Studio 54. We dated plenty of guys with great jobs, lots of cash, and no drug habits. Thank goodness. Network TV was and still is full of young, ambitious people. Drug use was common.

One evening after a long day of listening to Roger bellowing at us in a production meeting, a producer came into my office and offered me a plastic pen case and a line of cocaine. He loved to tease me about being a country bumpkin, so this was a double dog dare. I inhaled the whole line and felt like I was having a heart attack. I never tried coke again.

According to several books about the period, there was a

blizzard of "blow" a few floors above us, in the offices of the new show *Saturday Night Live*. Maybe it was the same in our offices and nobody shared with me, but I don't care. Keep that stuff away from me.

> Are you doing stupid things in your 20s? You're excused. But if you are experiencing addiction, no matter how old you are, get some help. Recovery is demanding, but it's one of the most powerful ways to start over. I've never met anyone in recovery who told me their lives were not improved after leaving their substance of choice behind. It's so hard to do, but it's worth it. If you've already tried, try again. This might be the right time for you.

All jobs end eventually, even the ones you wish you could hold onto forever. Sometimes a job ends when a company loses a big customer or is crushed by the competition. In network TV, sometimes it's plain corporate stupidity. Permanent doesn't really mean forever. It just means "as long as you are profitable."

NBC had signed a contract with David Letterman to host *The Late Late Show*, which aired after *Tomorrow Coast to Coast*. By the end of 1981 Letterman was angling for an earlier time slot, and ours looked appealing.

Roger had hired gossip reporter Rona Barrett, and NBC had guaranteed Tom and Rona equal time on TV, but they frequently fought with each other for primacy. By 1982 NBC finally had enough of this drama. *Tomorrow Coast to Coast* was cancelled, and Letterman took over.

I talked to my agent about possible next steps, and he said he had the perfect job for me. He sent me on an interview with the president of a startup news operation. They were looking for an executive producer for a show hosted by my agent's girlfriend. I was unaware that this was a setup. My agent wanted the network to replace the current executive producer, who he couldn't control with me, a girl, who would do what he told her to do. Probably.

This new "network" was unimpressive, with crappy equipment and a team of amateurs running the ancient studio cameras. While I was waiting to meet with the network president, I picked up *The Washington Post* and read that CBS had just hired George Merlis to revamp its perennially unsuccessful show, the *CBS Morning News.*

I decided a little subterfuge of my own was in order.

I used the visitor phone to call CBS and set up an interview with Merlis for the following week. My interview with the new network my agent wanted me to work for had gone well, and I was offered the job, but I turned it down. My sights were already set on CBS. I would not be working with the Chicken Noodle Network—CNN. At least, not yet.

 **Have you ever turned down a job offer? You may not always pick the right horse to ride. It's OK. Learn what you can, wherever you land. Be nice to all the horses. You may need to ride one of the old ones later on.**

I did. You'll see later in the book.

George hired me as an associate producer for the *CBS Morning News with Diane Sawyer and Bill Kurtis.* I was thrilled to start over again in TV, this time with a job at the "Tiffany Network" home of my hero, Walter Cronkite. But I was about to get a lesson in survival in network TV news.

When George introduced me to the show's senior producer, she looked at me and asked, "Are you Jeannie Edmunds from NBC?"

"Yes."

Then she said, "George, I want to talk to you before you hire anyone else." She turned around and walked out of the room. George and I just looked at each other. But he didn't withdraw the job offer, thank goodness.

Turns out this senior producer, the woman who would become my boss in a few days, was engaged to the man I had been dating for the last year. She had found some of my clothes in his apartment. I had no idea he had anyone else in his life. Both of us broke up with him, and somehow, we maintained a professional relationship, though it was a bit awkward. Fortunately, it was over soon. I was transferred to the Washington, DC, bureau. I don't know if she had anything to do with it, but I didn't care. I loved working for CBS and I had had enough of New York City.

**Could you handle working for someone who had it in for you? Why should that stop you from succeeding in your career? You have options: Talk it out, use a third party to mediate it, or ignore it.**

# Chapter 6
## Fixing Things

The Friday before I would start the job in DC, I had dinner with a *Morning News* producer, a woman in her early 30s who would share a cubicle with me (and sometimes compete with me) for the best guest bookings. We bonded over the fact that we'd both graduated from the University of Texas. I mentioned that I thought the Washington-based Sunday morning program *Face the Nation* needed a shakeup.

"How many times can you book Bob Dole, for heaven's sake? The show is boring, inside the Beltway, and irrelevant," I'd said, not realizing I might be digging my professional grave with such loose talk.

When I reported to work Monday, it didn't take long to discover that this producer, who'd pretended to be my ally, had repeated my comments to the Executive Producer of *Face the Nation*.

News travels fast, gossip travels faster.

 **Keep your own counsel when you're the new person in an organization. It's tempting, especially for women, to connect through shared confidences. Be friendly, but don't open the kimono too wide.**

At that time (and to some extent today) the Sunday shows were engineered to make news in the corridors of power in DC and on Wall Street. The only audience that seemed to matter were the three branches of government, *The New York Times*, and *The Washington Post*.

Betrayal aside, I stood by my observations about the program we all called "*Face*."

Two years later, ironically, I was hired as the producer of *Face the Nation* after the esteemed old-school newsman George Herman retired. Lesley Stahl would replace him in the anchor chair while she maintained her role as White House correspondent.

Every new TV show is a startup. Whenever a program hires a new anchor, the staff, the sets, and the programming can change, too. We redesigned the set and the graphics, giving the show a fresh look, but the biggest adjustment we made was in our selection of guests and topics.

The new Executive Producer, Karen Sughrue, and Lesley put their own imprimatur on the program. Karen was extremely capable and a great role model for me, because she was determined yet easygoing, and Lesley had a great deal of confidence in her. They wanted to "break the mold of all politics, all the time" as Karen put it. We leveraged Lesley's seniority and her role as the first female anchor to take on more current societal issues, women's issues, plus sports and entertainment. We covered the debut of the contraceptive sponge, a controversy over the sponsorship rights of Black athletes and produced a segment with Boy George for a show on androgyny, a hot topic in the '80s. We also included more women reporters in the roundtables at the end of the program.

After we taped our programs on Sundays, we had coffee and bagels with our guests and, as it usually works in Washington, we'd learn a lot more about the "story behind the story" after we were off the air. I met then-Senator Joe Biden, Dr. Anthony Fauci, lots of members of Congress and White House staffers, and yes, Senator Bob Dole, who was delightful. I could see why they booked him so many times in the past: He was a candid politician, a rare juxtaposition.

Lesley and I didn't always agree on the questions we'd collaborate on for her interviews, but she was gracious, and extremely generous. Soon after I'd arrived in Washington, I had met and fallen in love with Doug Apostol, a handsome, brilliant, law school grad, and during my second year at *Face the Nation* we were planning our wedding. Lesley hosted an elegant engagement dinner for us in her home in Northwest Washington, adding several of her high-powered Washington friends to the guest list. The Reagan administration's point man on nuclear issues, Ken Adelman, was seated at our table. Doug was looking for a way out of his law firm and he was keen to work on nuclear non-proliferation. This was a rare opportunity for him to meet influential people in that field.

He didn't get any job leads at that party (rookie), but it opened his eyes to the possibilities of networking through my work at CBS. This is how it goes at Washington social events. Even your own engagement party can open doors you could later walk through—if you knew how.

Lesley, her husband, Aaron, and Larry King all attended our wedding in June 1987. We were married in George Washington's church in Alexandria, Virginia, notable for its creaky old floors and the absence of air-conditioning.

It was a beautiful wedding, but the unbearable, swampy weather made it a miserable start to what would eventually become a troubled nine-year marriage. Standing in that church in the boiling afternoon heat, staring at the flickering candles while the preacher read from his notes, I heard nothing but the pounding of my heart telling me something wasn't right. But I was 33, and I was over the single life. I was all in, and I was willful. Even though we had already started to have problems in our relationship, I was certain I could fix whatever needed fixing, in him, or in me. I was ready to start over, as a wife.

> **Sometimes things just don't fit. No harm, no foul. You can't change other people. And they can't even change themselves if they're not ready. You'll know when to move on. You can't ignore your intuition forever.**

This lesson in listening to your gut became clear to me in business, too. In 2011, I would find myself in a management job with a medium-size business. It was not a great fit. The company paid me very well, and I loved the people, the products they sold, and my boss, but there was a mismatch between my strengths and interests and theirs.

> **Square peg, round hole, big salary. Is it worth the misery? It's great to stretch and take on challenges, but overreach is not always the best strategy. Aim for the skies but recognize your limitations. If you need retraining, a mentor, a lateral move, ask for it, before it's too late.**

In prior jobs, my skills, experience, and ability to learn quickly had always helped me rise up and overcome any professional challenge I might face. I was a Jill of all trades, but that was one job I was not going to master. Losing that job forced me to face the fact that no matter how talented I am or how much people enjoy working with me, I can't say yes to everything. When my friend and former colleague recommended me for the position, I should have done more homework on the company's expectations for the role.

Getting fired hurts, especially when the person firing you is the person who brought you in. It feels like such a betrayal. But as in relationships and marriages, they can train you, but they can't change you, and as an employee, you're not going to change them either.

This terrible experience forced me to reckon with my weaknesses, and helped me recommit to what really mattered to me professionally:

1. Being creative
2. Doing meaningful work
3. Surrounding myself with good people

The message was clear: I'd have to be Chief Executive Officer of my career and my life. Whether it's a blessing or a curse, I finally realized I have the heart, soul, and creative energy of an entrepreneur.

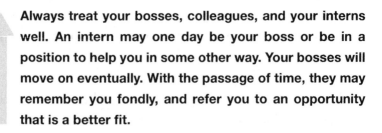

**Always treat your bosses, colleagues, and your interns well. An intern may one day be your boss or be in a position to help you in some other way. Your bosses will move on eventually. With the passage of time, they may remember you fondly, and refer you to an opportunity that is a better fit.**

# Chapter 7
# Overseas Adventure with CNN and the US Foreign Service

DC, 1991. Doug, my new husband, was restless. A junior associate at a large law firm in DC, he had a stellar pedigree: Stanford, the Fletcher School of Law and Diplomacy, Harvard Law, all on his own academic merit. But big law, especially tax law, was crushing his soul. He hadn't made any inroads into the arms control field, though he was still interested.

He had traveled around the world after law school and spoke Russian like a native. I urged him to take the Foreign Service test. For several years he resisted, saying he didn't want to get stuck in an embassy, stamping visas. With few exceptions, first-tour Foreign Service Officers have to work behind bullet-proof glass like bank tellers, interviewing locals about their reasons for coming to the United States and stamping their visas if they're approved. That didn't appeal to him, and I couldn't blame him.

Doug moved from his large firm to a boutique law firm

in the Georgetown section of DC. The partners were all very accomplished and supportive, but after three years he'd only worked on two seemingly endless cases: one suing the government of Iran over seized assets and the other opposing Native American tribes in a commercial dispute.

He finally had enough. He was ready to start over.

He took the Foreign Service test, passed the written and the orals, and then after he jumped through all the other hoops, he was sworn in with 200 other Foreign Service Officers in a solemn ceremony on the sixth floor of the State Department. We were given our first assignment: Seoul, Korea. I had a great job at the time, running a documentary unit at the Library of Congress. But I knew I would enjoy living overseas again, and I was thrilled we would be starting over in Asia, in a country neither of us had ever visited.

I had left the US for the first time when I was fifteen, spending the summer with a family in Asunción, Paraguay. Since then, I've always considered myself at home abroad. Doug was an inveterate traveler too, and he was as eager to start living overseas as I was.

I'd taken Doug's last name, considering myself a traditional wife, following her husband's career wherever it took him. There was no doubt in either of our minds that this move was right for him. I was just along for the ride, with plenty of fringe benefits: black diplomatic passports, embassy parties, socializing with prominent local families. But I never imagined the doors that would swing open for me, too. Sometimes life rewards you when you pull up your roots, especially when you put your career on hold to benefit your partner.

**What would you do? If you had no kids and a job you loved, and your partner had an offer to start over in another city, another country, how would you make your decision? It's the 21st century. Take turns. Their new opportunity may derail your career. But it could also create opportunities for you.**

Do I ever wonder how my career would have turned out if I had stayed? Not really, because life's detours make sense when you look in the rear-view mirror. Moving to Korea introduced me to exciting new opportunities in television. Didn't see that coming.

In a foreign country, adventures find you whether you want them or not. A journey overseas renders you as helpless as a toddler. You get to experience the world with "beginner's mind."

The unexpected is part of your routine. You get lost. Without language skills in a new country, you have no choice: You surrender to fate. Your success and sometimes your safety, depends on the kindness of strangers. Inconvenience, last-minute cancellations and alterations of itinerary, the occasional rip-offs, and surprise encounters with natives—and with other travelers—have made my journeys memorable and rewarding. They've been foundational to my personal growth.

**If you can make a living from a strong WiFi signal and a laptop, there are plenty of opportunities to try working for a few months at a time in other states, or other countries. Or maybe your company has a satellite office or a partner you could work with for a while. Professional**

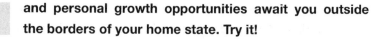

**and personal growth opportunities await you outside the borders of your home state. Try it!**

CNN had a bureau but no reporter in Seoul, so a few months after our relocation, I faxed my résumé and headshot to Eason Jordan, the senior vice president of international newsgathering. After checking my references and interviewing me, he hired me as a reporter. This would be my first time on camera. I'd need new hair and a new wardrobe. But I was ready for the high wire act of putting my face and words on camera in front of a worldwide audience. I was ready for this reinvention.

I filed three to four stories a week for two years, and CNN became yet another corporate logo for my growing, eight-lane resume. Starting up and starting over is my jam.

I reported from the DMZ, from Cheju Island, Pusan, Taejon, and all over Seoul. I covered the election of Kim Young Sam vs. Kim Dae Jung, and flew around in a helicopter with the sitting president, while Doug was stuck behind a teller window in the embassy, listening to PhDs who claimed they wanted visas to come to the US and work as chicken pluckers in Alabama. Every few weeks the "Why I need a visa" stories would change, but the most memorable was the week of the highly educated chicken pluckers. They must have had relatives in the US who'd told them about the job openings in Alabama's chicken processing plants.

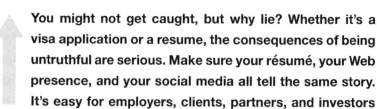

**You might not get caught, but why lie? Whether it's a visa application or a resume, the consequences of being untruthful are serious. Make sure your résumé, your Web presence, and your social media all tell the same story. It's easy for employers, clients, partners, and investors**

to check you out before they ever ask for references. And trust works both ways. Do your homework on a potential future employer, partner, or investor. As Ronald Reagan said about Gorbachev's promises to reduce Russia's nuclear arsenal, "Trust, but verify."

As an embassy wife who worked for CNN, I built a firewall between what I heard at diplomatic functions and what I learned as a journalist. That boundary was tested on July 5, 1993, when an explosion rocked the Hyatt Hotel in Itaewon, near the Yongsan Army base.

The CNN international desk editor had read the news on the English language wire service reports out of Seoul, and he called me at 3:00 a.m. to tell me to hurry over to the hotel. A few minutes later Doug got a call from the Embassy. Even though he was a junior officer at the time, it was all hands on deck.

We drove over to the blast site together, each with our own mission. The Secret Service was investigating, alongside other US and Korean agencies, and the embassy people stayed close by them. I scrambled to find sources willing to go on the air with me.

Bill Clinton had been scheduled to arrive at the Hyatt in a few days for an official visit, and the White House Communications Agency had already loaded in all the secure communications gear they normally travel with. Now it would have to all be moved.

The military organized relay teams of soldiers to help carry thousands of pounds of the sensitive equipment down sixteen flights of stairs in the dark. The blast had destroyed the electrical panels in the hotel. There was a gaping hole in the lobby floor near one of the jewelry stores. I was excited to go live with the story, and I did my best to quickly dig up reliable information for my reports, but during each live shot I wondered if more blasts would occur while I was on the air. I told you, I'm no hero. I like safe assignments.

A representative from a competing hotel was circulating among the press corps, saying how "unfortunate" it was that President Clinton had chosen the Hyatt and not his (rival) hotel. My bureau chief, Mr. Yoon, informed me that it was not unheard of for Korean companies to sabotage each other, and this angle was worth investigating.

I did a little digging, confirming with some sources that there were people in the US government who believed the explosion might have been an act of corporate sabotage. I filed a story, knowing it would be controversial. That evening I hopped a plane to Hong Kong for a meeting with Ted Turner and other CNN executives who were traveling in the region.

While I was away, the embassy brass interrogated Doug about my story.

"Where is she getting her information? Have you told her anything?" He swore he hadn't. To be sure, given his low rank as a first tour consular officer he probably knew less than I did. But this experience put us both on notice.

Since I was on a diplomatic passport, the Korean government couldn't easily declare me "persona non grata" and kick me out of the country. They didn't hesitate to do this to some of my fellow foreign correspondents for stories they didn't like, but my black passport made me virtually untouchable.

CNN had always given me the freedom to develop my own stories unless there was breaking news. After the explosion I tried to focus on local Korean stories, avoiding reporting on bilateral relations unless there was breaking news. Some journalists might accuse me of going soft, but I never let a story go if I thought it had to be reported. I did end up pissing off Doug's bosses—as well as the Koreans—from time to time. It was a high wire act. But I wasn't there to make people like me: I had a job to do.

I had traveled elsewhere in Asia, but Korea was unlike anywhere I'd visited. Once, while driving my BMW around a traffic circle in Seoul, I asked my passenger, a ROK (Republic of Korea) Army colonel, why Koreans don't stay in their lanes.

"Oh, those white lines? That's only for people who are learning how to drive," he said.

One on one, the Koreans I met were charming: funny, sensitive, educated, and unabashedly emotional. Sometimes men would cry when *Arirang*, the national anthem, was played at a public event. My Korean women friends were opinionated, sassy, and very much like American women. I adored them.

While I was living in Korea, my old friend and CBS News colleague, Jack Kirby, asked if I would travel to the US for a couple of weeks to produce some TV interviews for him. I wouldn't appear on camera, so it was okay with my bosses in Atlanta.

After he had replaced me as producer of *The Larry King Show*, Jack had bounced around in the news business before landing at a TV station in the exurbs of Los Angeles, where he'd been impressed by the economics of infomercials. He described the local TV market opportunity as "a bunch of guys with wheelbarrows full of cash who can't spend it fast enough." Jack decided to start an infomercial company of his own, Direct America. He hired Bruce (now Caitlyn) Jenner to promote a line of home-fitness equipment, and now he wanted me involved in the production.

I took a short vacation from CNN, flew to California, and

met Bruce, his wife, Kris, and the Kardashian kids. I conducted interviews with people who were using an affordable, foldable treadmill called the PowerWalk Plus. This infomercial made Bruce and Kris a few million dollars, with a nice bonus for me when the show "rolled out." Rolling out a show allows you to reinvest most of the money you make on a production into more media buys on TV, radio, or digital, so you can sell even more products and make more money. It's called self-liquidating media. If a show "rolls out," you just keep pumping it like a high-flying stock on Wall Street, until the party's over.

Several months after that project, Jack called me again and asked me to work on another Bruce Jenner fitness product, a portable stair-stepper called Stairclimber Plus. This time my mission was to fly to Barcelona two weeks before the Olympics. I would identify a location to shoot the "wraps"—Bruce's on-camera appearances with the fitness equipment. A Barcelona sound stage wouldn't do: Jack wanted me to secure an Olympic venue.

Big brands pay millions of dollars just to have their signs displayed during the Olympic games. That didn't deter me. I figured I could slip into town a few days before the opening ceremony and get permission for our crew to take over an official Olympic venue, no problem. But Jack didn't want to pay a location fee. I assured him I'd get it done, even though I wasn't sure how I was going to do it.

**Sit for a moment and try to remember the most audacious thing you ever did. Do you remember how it felt when people noticed your courage? Sometimes it takes cojones to get things done. What's the worst that**

> **can happen? You get a door slammed in your face. Ask anyone in sales. Or an actor. Or a politician. Rejection sucks. But as meditation teachers will tell you, let those thoughts and fears float by like passing clouds. They can't hurt you. You've got this.**

I didn't realize it at the time, but these trips for Jack were laying the groundwork for me to eventually start another career—in infomercials.

I had never been to an Olympics, but I'd spent time in Barcelona and knew my way around the city. I did some research and uncovered a potential outdoor location: the Velodrome, where they host the cycling events. I decided to hunt down the head of the Velodrome to see if I could work out a deal.

I used every ounce of my Southern guile and Spanish language ability plus Bruce's status as a former Olympic gold medalist to persuade this distinguished, older gentleman in charge of the venue that we would be no trouble at all and would be in and out in a few hours.

Within two days I had his signature on a location agreement—at no charge—and we quickly flew the crew over to get it "in the can" before the Spaniards changed their minds.

I remember thinking at the time that Kris Jenner would make a great co-host: She was very attractive, with a bubbly personality and a lot of ambition. Who knew she was already on her path to building the Kardashian brand?

 **Does the idea of working with celebrities appeal to you? Ask yourself why. Do you think they will become your friends? It's possible. Read Justine Bateman's book**

*Celebrity*. It's a raw, honest account of how weird it is to walk out in public and have people recognize you, want something from you, think they know you. It's the price of fame.

The experience in Barcelona gave me the confidence to ask anyone for anything I needed, whenever I needed it. They might say "no," but you'll never know until you ask.

# Chapter 8
## Big Nose, New Career

Halfway into our two-year tour in Korea, a diplomat's wife told me about some auditions coming up at a Korean TV network. KBS was looking for an American woman to play an itinerant teacher in a period drama. By "American" they meant "big nose." The word in Korean is *ko-jaeng-i*, which, roughly translated, means "nose-y."

I sat in the chair across from the director, showed him my profile, and he told me "You are the one!" He offered the equivalent of $50 an episode and I didn't negotiate. I knew that if nothing else, this would be something to write home about.

 **Sometimes starting something new is just a side hustle. Sometimes that side hustle is short-term, and a novel experience, even if it doesn't turn into a career.**

We taped the show on Saturdays in a small fishing village about an hour from Seoul. The production designers built elaborate sets depicting Korea under Japanese occupation in the early 1900s. Being on set was like stepping into the pages of a history book.

The production crew had refurbished a beautiful wooden tall ship. In my first scene I was filmed on the deck of this sailing vessel, staring at the shoreline as we slipped into the harbor at sunrise. Dressed in a heavy, dark, wool dress, with a wide-brimmed velvet hat and soft black leather shoes with tall chunky heels, I had to walk down the gangplank and enter the village surrounded by Koreans in white robes, with tall black scholars' hats.

I was completely out of my comfort zone, and it was thrilling. I couldn't understand what anyone around me was saying, and it was all I could do to keep from laughing at myself—I was sure viewers were embarrassed for me when they saw me on TV trying to speak Korean. Thank goodness I had an interpreter for my CNN reporting. I'd wanted to study the language, but it would have taken years to become proficient enough to conduct a news interview in Korean.

The director only spoke a few words of English. When I disembarked from the ship, I didn't know where I was supposed to go or how I was supposed to get there. I stepped off the gangplank, and my clunky Victorian heels sank into the sand. The director pointed at me and shouted, "You! Go there!"

I lifted my hoop skirt and ran up the hill toward the only one of the huts that was surrounded by lights and camera gear. The crew and all the extras laughed so hard they had to stop production so everyone could catch their breath. One of my fellow actors leaned over and whispered to me, "You no run, you walk."

Take two: I still didn't understand my motivation, but I walked this time, and since the director yelled "Cut-uh!" at the end, I assumed I did it correctly. Inside the hut I met Ha Hee-Ra, the Julia Roberts of Korea. I was playing the role of her beloved English teacher who had returned from America, concerned her student was getting herself in trouble. At one point I had to ask her *"Egi kachisumnika, Sangsun?"* (Are you pregnant?)

This soap opera had a long and successful run in Korea, but my character was mercifully written out of the show after the sixth episode. They were probably tired of filming me reading the script lines I had taped to her skirt or watching me sneak glances at my hand where I had written more dialogue.

Today if I meet Koreans of a certain age and mention the name of the show, *Mawndong* and the famous star, Ha Hee-Ra, they either remember watching it or they run to the Korean video store to try to rent it. My dad, bless him, watched all six episodes I appeared in, even though he didn't speak Korean either. There was no closed captioning on the videos I sent him.

**Are you itching to raise your profile by appearing on TV? Be prepared. The more visible you are, the more vulnerable you become to critics, competitors, and trolls. Consider the risk/reward.**

One day, in my main job as the CNN reporter in Seoul, I attended a press conference at the Blue House, the White House of Korea.

Here I was, the lonely little girl from a place most people never heard of, sitting in a press conference with the president of a foreign country. Soon I would go on TV and report to millions of people around the world.

I was daydreaming about this when President Kim Young Sam looked straight at me and asked, "Don't the ladies in the foreign press corps have a question?" I was startled, but I took the bait and asked him something I knew he didn't want to answer, about his response to the latest provocations by the North Koreans at the DMZ.

After the news conference he came up to me and smiled.

"That was a good question you asked me."

"Thank you, Mr. President," I said. "I noticed you didn't answer."

"You know I can't answer that. I just wanted to let you know I saw you on that KBS drama Saturday night," he said.

"You did? What did you think of my Korean?" I asked.

Long pause. "Well, people used to talk like that in those days," he said.

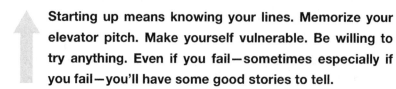

**Starting up means knowing your lines. Memorize your elevator pitch. Make yourself vulnerable. Be willing to try anything. Even if you fail—sometimes especially if you fail—you'll have some good stories to tell.**

My time in Korea was full of adventure, travel, politics, news, accolades and entertainment. I never wanted it to end. But the last few months of our tour there felt like the beginning of the end of our marriage.

With a short time left before we were to ship out, for the first time in my life I woke up feeling depressed. For three straight days I felt one-dimensional, heavy—I couldn't get out of bed. One night I looked across the seemingly vast distance that separated Doug and me on our king-sized bed and I knew it was over, but I wasn't ready to accept it. My heart was breaking, bit by bit. I didn't know what to do.

Doug had been spending a lot of time with his single friends after work, and one night he didn't come home at all. Probably spending time with the famous Korean blind masseuses in taffeta prom dresses, or if not, maybe he was in a late-night coffee shop with one of the Korean girls from the embassy who were dazzled by his height and his Harvard degree.

By the fourth day, I had had enough of my pity party. One of the Korean president's top advisors invited me out to a club for dinner. Doug would be out for the evening with his friends, so I decided to go out and try to have a good time.

**Starting something new can mean letting something else go. That can feel like letting go of a lifeline. It is. Get used to it. Draw a picture of your bravest moment or write a few paragraphs about it and frame it. Notice how you react to it now, and six months from now.**

# Chapter 9
# On the Road Again...
# Marriage on the Rocks

Doug and I were headed back to Washington in 1994 for language and cultural training. He would perfect his Russian, and I would study Ukrainian in advance of our next posting to the US embassy in Kiev the following spring. Cramming a new language into your head after forty is a challenge—a real reinvention—but as with all language learning, it requires a suspension of disbelief, and an ability to guess meanings in context. Having already studied several languages, I was ready for it. Korean had eluded me. I was ready to conquer Ukrainian with the help of the State Department's total immersion language training: five days a week, six hours a day.

We had a few weeks of government-funded R&R before our training would begin, so Doug and I took a camping trip to Hawaii and Alaska. We thought spending time in nature might help us get our groove back. Before we were married Doug had bought me my first backpack and introduced me to the pleasures of camping and cooking in nature. He had helped me climb my first mountain, Mount Kinabalu in Borneo. I did okay for someone who had never climbed before, though I did want to stop and rest at every switchback. The last half-mile I was on my hands and knees, crawling toward to the lodge at 11,000 feet. We made it before dark, and I collapsed in front of the fireplace, oxygen-deficient, ashen-faced, and hungry, but I finally felt like a real hiker. We made it to the bunkroom, and Doug set his alarm for 3:00 a.m. so he could trek the last mile to the peak the next morning to watch the sunrise. I couldn't get started, I had no energy left, and since it involved ropes and more climbing and getting up in the wee hours, I passed.

Our campsites in Hawaii were perfect. There's nothing like placing your sleeping bag on top of the Hawaiian dirt, feeling the "mana" of the land. The vibrations of the ground, even on the volcanically inactive Islands of Maui and Kauai, lulled me to sleep and gave me beautiful dreams. I don't think I've slept that soundly since.

The places we visited were under-populated, well-maintained, and Hawaii-beautiful. On Maui, we camped near the Seven Sacred Pools, sleeping under a beautiful banyan tree on a hill above the ocean. On Kauai, we camped on the north shore of the island, on the south shore near Poipu, and in the Waimea Valley.

Alaska was the next stop on our farewell-to-marriage tour. We camped on a ridge facing Mount McKinley in Denali National Park. It was June and at midnight the sky was still light, a deep dusky rose with the frosted peaks clearly visible in the moonlight. I wish I still had the photos from that trip; I left everything behind in the divorce. But my mental screenshot of that magnificent view is tucked away among my happiest memories.

I put on an eyeshade to try to get some sleep, but I couldn't let my guard down in grizzly territory. The training video they made us watch at the park headquarters had terrified me, and we had spotted a few bears on the bus ride into the backcountry. I was sure we were going to confront a mama bear before dawn. I wouldn't even eat a breakfast bar near the tent, I was so paranoid.

The evening passed without incident. The breathtaking view, clean air, and the adventure took our minds off our troubles for a while.

**Humans are drawn to the nature, especially when we need renewal. The beauty, the silence, the harmony, the timelessness. Nature provides a sanctuary for you to contemplate your most important life decisions. If you're thinking about starting over, go somewhere in nature and just stand or sit quietly. Turn off your phone. Open your mind. And listen. Nature heals, and sometimes reveals things you already know to be true, whether you're ready to accept them or not.**

We drove to Talkeetna and hired a pilot to fly us over the Mount McKinley base camp. We weren't technical climbers, so we didn't land; we just enjoyed the spectacular view. Add Alaska to your itinerary one day. I can't possibly do it justice without photos. It is unimaginably beautiful.

Back to Anchorage and down the Kenai Peninsula, we passed rivers so many shades of green they looked like liquid forests. We spent a couple of nights in Homer, where we took a boat out to some islands to see the puffins. They were adorable, much smaller than I'd expected so not very easy to see from the boat without binoculars. Though we were entertained and enjoyed our time together, we were near the end of our life as a couple, and we both knew it.

We drove up to Fairbanks, where we sat outdoors in a hot tub and sipped champagne as a surprising summer snow fell around us. Heading back south, we drove through Wrangell-St. Elias National Park, the most breathtaking national park I've ever visited. We winched ourselves across a raging river in a bucket to visit the abandoned mining town of Kennecott. In the car on the way back to our campsite the sun was slowly sinking behind the mountain peaks. The repetitive crunching of tires along the gravel road lulled me into a catnap when suddenly, the fox appeared—a chimera.

That fox can appear the second I close my eyes and occasionally shows up during meditation, even today. It is the perfect animal guide for someone like me. The fox's wisdom is said to include:
- ▲ Shapeshifting
- ▲ Cleverness
- ▲ Observational skills
- ▲ Persistence
- ▲ Ability to observe the unseen.

I've seen the fox with tears in her eyes. I've seen her looking at me intently with different facial expressions. But I'd never seen her do what she did that afternoon in Alaska.

In my dream state, the fox shook her head back and forth. I shouted "No!" and woke up to see a logging truck headed straight toward us. Doug had nodded off as well. He woke up, swerved, and missed the truck by a fraction of a second.

Even with all the natural beauty and the heart stopping near-death experience that might have brought us closer together, our marriage was running on fumes. I don't know why, or how, we held on so long.

> **When something in your private life isn't working, you can always focus on your career. But has that really solved anything? Might it be time to have the hard conversations about starting over in your relationship? Or starting over without it?**

Back in DC, Doug and I tried once again to make our marriage work. He was the quiet one. I always needed to know what lay beneath his silence, and to him, that probing was just too intrusive.

We spent most of the year living in Shirlington, an area that has housed government employees and other Washington workers for decades. For nine months it was a time of reinventing ourselves as students. We went to language and cultural immersion classes all day and came home to second-hand furniture from Ikea via Goodwill. Then we gave everything away when we left, with a plan to start our marriage over again, overseas.

Doug and I headed to Kiev in February 1996, realizing our relationship was fragile but still not wanting to fully admit it to each other, or to ourselves. Our regret and resignation burdened us individually, but it was too traumatic to talk about.

After we'd settled into our beautiful townhouse in the garden city of the former Soviet Union, Jack Kirby called from California with another business opportunity. He asked me to join his new infomercial company as a partner. I would spend three weeks in LA and return to Kiev once a month. CNN's Moscow Bureau Chief was the senior correspondent in the region and since she outranked me, I hadn't had much airtime. Still, I wasn't ready to give up this gig, so I agreed to Jack's offer on a trial basis.

> **Sometimes you jump, sometimes you're pushed, and sometimes somebody throws you a life preserver. You may not think you're ready for something new, but what if you had an offer that's too attractive to turn down? What if your partner encourages you to take it? How will you decide? Financial freedom isn't everything, but it can give you a soft landing.**

For 18 months I commuted between LA and Kiev, or London, or wherever else Doug and I chose to meet. After so many international flights I was so sleep deprived I ended up in the emergency room. Extreme, I know, but extreme was my normal in those days. I'm sure the ER doctor assumed I was on drugs. I was completely disoriented and incoherent. His remedy— Nyquil—knocked me out and I slept for 12 hours. When I woke up, I felt fine. I was cured.

> **International travel takes a toll on your body and your mind, even if you're young. Want to be at the top of your game? Don't land and go to your meeting after crossing eight times zones. No bueno. Take a day to rest.**

I had hoped my new, lucrative job in California would give us a chance to plan for our future together. Maybe time apart would help us appreciate each other again. Meeting for mini-vacations in different European cities would rekindle the romance, I thought. But one autumn night in Prague, drifting arm in arm across the

Charles Bridge after a tearful conversation at dinner, I watched other couples as they embraced. I turned to Doug and said, "You know, this feels a little like walking down the aisle in reverse." He was silent.

In October 2006, I flew from LA to Kiev to make one last attempt to save our marriage. Jack had encouraged me to stay as long as I needed, to fix things. For two weeks Doug barely spoke to me. He was often pensive, but this was troubling.

Finally, the night before I was set to leave, he said it.

"I don't know if I love you anymore."

He may not have known, but I knew.

The next day, on the plane ride back to LA, the stranger seated next to me told me everything I needed to hear, after she noticed me crying and I'd told her my story. Her words were a gift. That conversation gave me permission to do what I needed to do. I was ready to make the break. Almost.

> **When you've made a promise to stay married until one of you dies; when you've sworn an oath to wear a badge or a uniform; when you've signed a contract committing you to something long-term, how do you make your exit with your dignity and honor intact? Sometimes you just can't go on, and that's okay. There's always a way out. Be honest, make a fair offer in exchange for your freedom. And try to keep lawyers out of it if you can. It's so much better when neither side thinks they're getting screwed.**

After nine years in a difficult marriage and after making the decision to leave, I felt like a captive bird let out of her cage. I bought a dozen tickets to the Brazilian carnival party at the LA

Palladium and took a bunch of friends with me. We danced the samba till the wee hours. I even made out with a guy I had just met. I listened to Anita Baker at full volume in my little sanctuary on Point Dume in Malibu and reveled in my new freedom as a single woman in my early 40s, with a sexy convertible and a substantial income.

My mother called me a few weeks after the Brazilian bacchanalia and said she had run into a woman who used to babysit for me when I was in elementary school. She had told mom she was working with a Kundalini yoga instructor who wanted to do an infomercial, and mom thought I could help her.

I flew to Vancouver for a weekend yoga retreat with my babysitter's client, and it was wonderfully cathartic. She got my chakras spinning and claimed she could read a deep purple aura around me as I was leaving the retreat to head back to LA. A violet aura is associated with the crown chakra, the locus of your intuition. I sensed a change was imminent.

That teacher never did an infomercial, but the weekend was so sublime, my heart was completely open. I knew I was primed for a new chapter in my life. I came home and filed for divorce.

 **Try as hard as you can, in business and in relationships, and if it doesn't work out, face the facts. Will it be okay? Who knows? Sometimes you just have to trust the universe. In Arabic *iinaha maktouba* means "It is written." The unexpected, and sometimes the miraculous, can happen when you end something that isn't working for you. So long as we're alive, all endings are also the beginning of something new.**

The divorce was regrettable, but inevitable. It was time for both of us to start over.

# Chapter 10
## A Detour: Infomercials

I was one of four partners in Jack Kirby's infomercial company, Direct America. Traditional advertisers disparage people who produce infomercials, known in the industry as Direct Response TV (DRTV). We were the rogues of the ad business, but our company made millions. We didn't need Madison Avenue cred.

Direct America was acquired by National Media Corporation. As the newly formed Quantum TV, we produced DRTV shows—infomercials—on our own, and some in partnership with Guthy Renker, a righteous company in an industry full of sharks and sleazy operators. One of our joint productions was for a bucking bronco–type product called the Power Rider.

The pitchman was football legend Fran Tarkenton, who shared top billing with a trained elephant stomping around an outdoor mall. Only Jack would have thought of putting an elephant in a show where we were selling the dream of being skinny. Maybe the elephant was a subtle reminder of how you'd feel if you didn't buy the product to lose weight. Subliminal advertising.

We also shot and tested a show for the Treadclimber Plus with one of the original Charlie's Angels. The product was the first treadmill with a split tread that moved up and down as you walked. Cool product. Really expensive.

The "talent" was very well paid for just a few of days of rehearsal and shooting. No doubt she put her career on the line by getting involved in something as down-market as an infomercial. But the camera doesn't lie. She just couldn't convey any enthusiasm for the product. We tested the show, but the response was weak.

> **If you're trying to growth hack your business by using celebrities or influencers consider this: Are they really a good match, or are you wowed by their high profile? Does the celeb have a life story or a passion that ties into what you're selling? Potential customers can sense faux enthusiasm, especially on video, even on the small screen of a mobile phone. The camera lens is like a polygraph, and audiences know the truth.**

There are lots of ways to "tweak" an infomercial or an e-commerce website, but only one way to succeed: Find the winning combination of product, host, price, testimonials, offers, and upsells—what you sell the customer after they've agreed to buy the main product.

Before the English pitchman Mick Hastie made the Magic Bullet a household-must-have blender, he was our super successful products "demo guy" at Quantum TV. We sent Mick to an aquarium in California to mop up after a dolphin show, proving the Magic Mop was the world's best kitchen mop. Mick and the DR strategists who wrote that show, Brady Caverly and Jeff Clifford, knew exactly which sell words, which demos, and which offers would get people to buy our products. They were DR geniuses.

One day I recall Jack Kirby popping into my office to ask if I thought anyone would buy a grill from George Foreman. I said, "Hell no," and he agreed. We lost that opportunity. Yet I have bought and enjoyed a couple of George Foreman grills since his infomercial hooked me. I know all the tricks and yet I still whip out my credit card if I identify with the dream that's being sold.

> **We all have our missed opportunities, the stories in our love lives of the one who got away, the investments we didn't make that took off, the product we thought of that someone else brought to market first. Sylvia Plath, the author of *The Bell Jar*, wrote about choices, and the consequences of not choosing. If you don't choose, right or wrong, you lose. Shoulda, coulda, woulda.**

Roger Ailes, my horrible boss at NBC, used to say that TV *viewers* just wanted to know three things: how to get more money, more power, and more sex. TV *buyers* can be moved by those fundamentals, too, but there's a reason many infomercials are successful late at night, besides the low-cost media buy: Critical thinking is less engaged, and most people are more open to dreaming and projecting themselves into the content, imagining they'll get the same benefits they see people demonstrating on the screen. When you buy from TV or online, you may think you're buying a product, but what really gets you to open your wallet is the story and how it connects with you. You are primed for reinvention, just as your defenses are down. Maybe that's not such a bad thing.

> **Being persuasive isn't a bad thing. It's just sales. And it's also the key to leadership. Who wants to follow someone they don't believe in? This applies to startup founders, parents, marketers, job hunters, and founders pitching investors. Project confidence. Sell the dream. Know your audience and adjust your message accordingly.**

I understand why people get upset with infomercials. They're everywhere and they're obnoxious. They're repetitive, obviously selling every second, even in what appears to be casual conversation. But traditional advertising, with its veneer of respectability, is selling you even as it entertains you or makes you feel good, so which is more insidious?

# Chapter 11
## The Magic of Starting Over

It was 1996, and I was feeling frisky after my yoga retreat in Vancouver. I was so ready for a fresh start. My girlfriend Andrea (my old pal from *Tomorrow Coast to Coast*) and I went to the annual New Year's Eve party hosted by a mutual friend in Beverly Hills. Our friend Alicia has had an enviable career/life. She was a director for *Entertainment Tonight* for more than 20 years, but she's never been an employee—always a freelancer. Her lifestyle drives her work: Make some money, save it, travel, rinse, repeat. She had the discipline to make this happen every few years, running with the bulls in Pamplona, riding horses with the migrating wildebeests in Africa, visiting friends in Samoa. The girl's got game. She knows how to start things up.

At midnight, as Alicia waved a magic wand over her guests for good luck, she tapped it on my shoulders and made a wish for me. Four months later that wish would come true.

I had lived with a roommate for a short time after my divorce, and then moved into a luxurious Balinese-style guest house on Zumirez Road in Malibu, a few doors down from Barbra

Streisand's compound. The lease came with a key to the private beach at Little Dume, just below Streisand's property.

Point Dume is a magical little peninsula. It's a microclimate with frequently foggy summer days and cool nights, and it's greener and more flower-filled than other parts of Malibu. The Point used to be the end of the earth from LA proper. It was inhabited in the 1930s and 1940s by teachers and firefighters—people who couldn't afford to live closer to town.

These days realtors are selling $10 million "tear downs." There are fewer and fewer of the first families who haven't sold and moved on. Some have managed to hang on to their homes, though, even after the devastating fires of 2018. The Point is an extraordinary healing place, never mind the periodic mudslides, earthquakes, and fires. Maybe that's why it's so restorative. Nature keeps renewing herself here.

My daily commute to Quantum TV in Encino was terrible, but the tradeoff was worth it. Though thousands of tourists jammed the Pacific Coast Highway in summer, Malibu still felt like a small town, and I felt I belonged there. My guesthouse was the perfect cocoon for one, plus dog. It was also the perfect love nest, but I had no love. I was alone.

Then, Alicia's New Year's Eve party magic finally produced some results: I fell in love. With someone from my past.

Flashback to 1985, Washington, DC. A political PR firm hired me to work on a project. One of their other vendors, Don Ringe, was a superstar Republican political ad guy. One night we went out for dinner (sort of a business meeting, could've turned into a date) but it was a disaster. I thought he was arrogant, he chain-smoked, and as they say west of the Pecos, he had a bad case of big behavior. He didn't like me, either.

In June 1987, one week after I'd married Doug, Don got married at his horse farm near Middleburg, Virginia. Although Don and I couldn't bear each other, we had several mutual friends. Some of them attended both weddings.

Ten years later, Don was going through a divorce and so was I. We both lived in Malibu, and mutual friends in several cities insisted that we get together.

"Are you kidding? I can't stand that guy. We're both getting divorced. That's all we have in common. No thanks," I said. Though he was reluctant to meet as well, he called me one night and we talked for an hour. We agreed to meet at Bambu, a local sushi bar. I saw him from across the room and went up to him. When I hugged him, to my surprise, I couldn't let go. It felt like something was tapping on my head, right in the middle of my crown chakra. Crazy.

 **Hello? When the universe sends you a message, pay attention.**

We sat at the sushi bar and talked about where we'd traveled in the past 10 years. He had quit smoking, spent a summer learning to blow glass and mellowed out. By the time dinner was over, I didn't want to go home. Two days later we went out again, this time for a walk along the Point Dume headlands.

"This is where you bring someone when you want to fall in love, Don Ringe," I said. "I hope it happens for you again." As we walked around the Point we saw a bride in a wedding dress standing on the cliff, having her photo taken. You couldn't make this up. We stopped and watched for a while. Both of us said we never wanted to get married again, though we did want to fall in love. Who could have predicted we'd fall for each other after that terrible first encounter, and a decade married to other people?

We walked up the hill to find my car had been towed (welcome to Malibu), so Don had to give me a ride home.

I moved in with him three months later.

By June I was pregnant and had a miscarriage in August. We were both devastated. We had always wanted a baby but were unable to with our previous spouses.

In December I gave him a tiny Christmas stocking with a new, positive pregnancy test in it. We were overjoyed, and hopeful we would finally be parents. Don had just turned 52, I was 44. The conversation on the plane from Kiev. The magic wand. The yoga retreat. Two pregnancies. It felt like we were destined to be together. Forever.

1998 was an El Niño year, and the waves were pounding Carbon Beach in front of Don's condo, where our much wealthier neighbors were David Geffen, Michael Eisner, and Larry Ellison. We all shared a view of the boiling, murky ocean that tore away the sand, leaving smelly brown seaweed on the shore.

Our whole building shook in the winds, day and night. I was extra hormonal and nervous. It was 11:59 on my biological clock, and I didn't want to risk having another miscarriage. My obstetrician said I needed to go on bed rest because of my aging insides. Since Don worked for himself and could live anywhere, we decided to move to San Francisco. Two of my brothers lived in the Bay Area, and Don had always wanted to live there again after he'd worked for KPIX early in his career.

I said goodbye to my life in infomercials and hello to a pampered "geriatric pregnancy" and eventually, stay-at-home mothering.

**First step in starting over? Look behind you. Someone from your past may have changed, and you probably have, too. Maybe it's time to reconnect.**

# Chapter 12
# A Personal Chef, A Nanny, and A Bourgeois Bay Area Lifestyle

San Francisco, 1998. We got sucked into the dotcom boom and invested in AOL, WebVan, Ask Jeeves, and a few other promising tech startups. Just before the bubble burst. We had a private chef, who we "needed to hire" when I was on bed rest due to some issues with my pregnancy. We also employed a housekeeper and, after our daughter was born, a nanny. So, a staff of three. And we lived in the heart of high-rent Pacific Heights. We were so, so bougie.

A few months after we became new parents, we were one of the first couples to get married in the newly renovated City Hall in San Francisco. The combined wedding/birth announcement included a photo of then-mayor Willie Brown, who married us, holding our baby. With the bride and groom on either side of him. Willie was a real gentleman, letting our drooling baby rest on the arm of his Brioni suit. (Fifteen years later, one of my brothers was seated next to Willie at the opening of the new

Jazz Center in San Francisco. He asked the former mayor if he'd remembered the marriage ceremony and holding Margaret. He said he'd never forgotten it. Such a politician).

Don and I were looking forward to working on a new startup together—you could call it our second startup—after the baby. We wanted to build a tech company. I was eager to get going, because the business world felt a lot more familiar than parenting. Margaret was well cared for by her nanny, Lisett, an experienced and devoted mom who seemed so much more capable of parenting her than I was. I can't believe I was so unsure of myself as a mother. I had read all the books, and the conflicting advice made me numb. So, I took the businesswoman's approach and hired a vendor. Ouch.

**Should you outsource certain aspects of your business? Hire only freelancers or consultants? Rely on outside experts to tell you how to run your company? These are important decisions with a lot of variables. Your startup company, your new adventure in life, is something you give birth to and nurture. Outside expertise is great, but in the end, you will know what's best. Identify your true north. Then use it to guide all of your decisions.**

Like many Bay Area residents caught up in the frenzy of Internet riches, we thought we had enough creative and business chops to be tech founders, not just shareholders. We bought a URL, iwantaction.com, hired a ridiculously expensive financial expert to help us write a business plan, and prepared to go out for funding.

We had no idea what we were doing.

iwantaction.com would drive donations and action tied to events in the news. For example, if a hurricane hit somewhere the Red Cross would order a direct response TV ad to drive people to donate on the Web. We would produce the ad and deliver it in 12–24 hours. His experience in political media and mine in news and direct response TV would make this startup successful, we thought.

Our timing for investment couldn't have been worse. Just as we were going out for our first investor meetings in 2001, a federal court declared Microsoft a monopoly, tech stocks cratered, and kept declining that entire year. Investors were spooked. Oh, and those Internet stocks? We bought high, sold low, and took our losses.

We gave up on tech, but not startups. I eventually made my way back there, after a few detours.

We decided to head back to Washington so Don could develop business with new political media clients. His unconventional approach to promoting Republican candidates had earned him a national reputation as one of the most creative ad men in the US. But now there were few moderate Republicans left. He wanted to explore the possibility of doing only issue advocacy work, and helping moderate Democrats, if they'd hire him after he'd worked for the other side.

I would stay at home with Margaret, and try my best to be a capable, full-time mom. En route to DC, we made a detour to Little Switzerland, North Carolina, where we had rented a house for the summer.

Don owned some land in Burnsville, about 20 minutes away. He had bought it a decade earlier when he was attending the

Penland School of Craft in Spruce Pine, studying glassblowing. At the time he was recovering after an angioplasty, considering retiring to become a full-time artist. He loved the hot furnace and the flames and the alchemy of blowing glass. For him it was the perfect escape after years of promoting blowhard politicians. But it could never replace his lust for politics. It was his calling. He couldn't stay away from the action.

**Are you letting your past confine you, or define you? Ask yourself this. Is your current life's work really your calling? Or just where you ended up because that's what you studied in school? Or your parents pushed you into it? Or you don't think you're capable of doing anything different? In the words of Steve Jobs, who died at 56, "Your time is limited, so don't waste it living someone else's life."**

The vegetation on the property in the mountains outside of Burnsville had matured since we'd last visited the area. But the large boulders were still there, plopped like giant pewter marbles in the path of the bold, rushing creek. On this summer vacation, Don planned to spend the mornings cutting trails and pruning the eight-foot rhododendrons, while I would join a local mom group and enjoy my days as a late-in-life parent.

One afternoon we pitched a tent by the creek, testing our resolve to build a house there and try to make a living working remotely. The creek was up and it was so loud we could barely hear each other. We started to wonder if having a house would be a dream, or a disaster.

That night, with only the thin GoreTex of the tent protecting me from the elements, a huge snake slithered up my side, from my ankles to my neck and head, trying to find a place to get warm, I suppose.

We called the realtor the next day to sell the land and reverted to plan A, living near the Potomac. Neither of us really wanted to live there anyway—we both disliked cold winters— so the snake was a convenient excuse.

We had tickets to fly out of Charlotte airport September 15, 2001. The morning of September 11, we were hundreds of miles from the heartache and the horror, and watched helplessly as the towers fell, and the Pentagon smoldered on live TV. We considered returning to California, as far away from the East Coast as possible, but, like everyone else, we were confused, afraid, and paralyzed.

Within days, though, Don was called to Washington for meetings with a lobbying firm. They wanted to hire him right away. We were shocked that the engines of politics and business restarted so quickly, and a little disappointed we weren't heading West again.

We flew to DC together on the 15th as originally planned and moved into a townhouse in the Old Town section of Alexandria, Virginia, seven miles from the Pentagon. As we landed, the skies were eerily quiet and cornflower blue: Air traffic hadn't fully resumed, even though businesses had reopened. People were still shell-shocked, and we were not quite sure how our plan to re-establish our lives as a Washington political/media couple was going to work out.

And we thought that those were the worst days we'd ever have to live through!

A few months later business was great, but it was getting

cold. We longed for more sunny days in Southern California. Fortunately, a trade association hired Don to do a project he'd shoot in LA: a series of videos for college freshmen on the dangers of binge drinking. We kept our townhouse in Alexandria and rented a house in Malibu for the duration of the shoot and edit. We were so happy to be back in La La Land.

When the job was over, we decided to start over (again) and become permanent residents of the Golden State. We no longer had the will or the wardrobe to live in a cold climate. We leased a modern house overlooking the ocean in the hills above eastern Malibu. I loved that house. Some nights we could hear the waves in the distance, but in spring the winds whipped up the hillsides so fiercely it was hard to fall asleep. It was dramatic, and I felt so at home there. I wanted to buy it, but it was too far from Topanga, where Margaret would eventually go to school.

**When thinking about relocating, consider this: Are you running away? Or chasing a dream? Both are valid reasons to move. Staying put is almost always the safer choice, but if you're ready to for a change, make an extended visit to the area, if you can. If you're considering California, there are plenty of pros and cons. It's an exceedingly beautiful state. But it's not nirvana.**

"Believe or Leave" is the tag line for the BOL company, a meditation lifestyle brand that will always be one of my favorite clients. The founder believes that accepting the status quo is not an option if you're feeling restless. I agree. There's nothing worse than inertia.

When our daughter Margaret entered kindergarten at Topanga Elementary School, I took a full-time job as editor of a health magazine. I'd never worked in publishing, but I was ready to learn the business, and I wanted to add more writing and editing to my portfolio. The offices were upstairs in an old western style building in Topanga, across from the landmark—Flying Pig—a fat, pink papier-mâché pig perched atop a flagpole.

Starting up again, with a view of the pink pig from my office window, and the smell of bacon drifting up from the restaurant downstairs.

*Healthy Living* was the infomercial of magazines. The articles were thoughtful, well written, and professionally edited, but the advertisers provided some of the experts for our stories, and reviewed the copy before we went to press.

This practice was appalling to the journalist in me until I discovered that, for some magazines, the relationship between publishers and advertisers has always been cozy. Many magazines have no problem offering "editorial" in exchange for a certain amount of ad buy, so what's the difference?

The *Healthy Living* writers and editors had a lot of autonomy, but we were relying on our advertiser "partners" to provide us with substantiation that their claims were valid. The Food and Drug Administration doesn't approve supplements before they go on the market, so unless the companies make unsubstantiated claims or the public reports adverse effects, they can sell their products anywhere.

The Federal Trade Commission controls what you can write about supplements, though, and it has fined people millions of dollars for making claims that are too aggressive. If you see "fortifies the digestive system" or "supports a healthy immune system," you'll know that language is dictated by the government watchdogs at the FTC.

Working for a small magazine meant a giant leap backward in salary, but I enjoyed editing, working with writers and photographers, and writing articles about natural health. We only had deadlines once a month, so it was a much more leisurely pace than radio or TV. Back in my happy place of work, I was excited to come to the office every day. I liked the staff and the freelancers we hired, and it was an honor to help some of the best companies in natural health—New Chapter, Barleans, Gaia Herbs, and many others—build their brands through our publication.

After six months on the job, the publisher asked me to edit an integrative medicine book: *Dr. Katz's Guide to Prostate Health: From Conventional to Holistic Therapies*—current, reliable, and straightforward medical information, written by a highly regarded New York physician.

It was also a brilliant piece of content marketing for the supplements companies mentioned in the book. As with the magazine, this type of arrangement is not unusual. Popular alternative medicine books you may find in natural grocery stores, online, or in bookstores are sometimes the result of product-placement deals. They're not necessarily pay-to-play, but companies sometimes buy lots of copies of a book if they're mentioned favorably and frequently. Dr. Aaron Katz, who I greatly admire, had a reputation to protect, so he only wrote about supplements that he had personally used, or recommended to his patients.

The publisher of *Healthy Living* was a seasoned marketer. A few months after he promoted me to executive editor, he asked me to design a business publication to compete with the giant business-to-business tabloid, *Natural Foods Merchandiser*. *NFM* had been around for years, and the market for natural and organic products was growing rapidly. He saw a great market opportunity and gave me the editorial budget to try to compete.

I hired designers and writers, but I wrote most of the content and oversaw the creation, launch, and monthly publication of *Natural Health Retailer*. We distributed four issues, but most of the large natural products advertisers were already locked up by *NFM*. This is business intelligence we could have and should have gathered before we invested in printing four issues of our magazine. We were never able to secure enough ad revenue to support the magazine long term. This publishing startup folded after four months.

 **Does your startup have the right business model? Do you have enough funds to carry you across the great divide from where you are today to where you want to be? Plan. Gather and analyze your data. Make sure you have the right resources, both financial and human. Don't get stuck in analysis paralysis but do give yourself the gift of a good plan of action.**

*Healthy Living* magazine sent me to Sanoviv, a medical spa located in Rosarito, Mexico, owned the MLM supplements company USANA. The founder of USANA is an outspoken critic of conventional dentistry and has written books and articles about the dangers of mercury fillings. Sanoviv offers removal of mercury fillings, detoxing, colonics, dry brushing, and other alternative therapies that some people think are quackery. There is science behind some of these therapies, but I believe the placebo effect of having hands on, sympathetic humans around can heal you, too.

Sanoviv is built on the grounds of the former home of Levi Strauss, alongside a small modern hotel. There are classrooms, surgical suites and an extensive menu of medical procedures, too. I don't have any insights as to the efficacy of USANA supplements, but I was impressed by how the company integrated these therapies into their functional medicine practice at Sanoviv. It was a very hospitable, clean, and comfortable place to relax and renew.

*Healthy Living* also sent me to Expo West, the largest natural products expo in the world. It is held at the convention center in Anaheim, California, every March, and I've attended almost every year since 2005. One year I invited my friend Wendy Makkena, an actress with a deep commitment to healthy food and sustainable living.

Wendy has a lengthy list of acting credits, but most remember her as the shy nun in *Sister Act*. She's also had leading and recurring roles on Broadway, in network TV comedies and dramas, and a supporting role in *A Beautiful Day in the Neighborhood,* the 2019 film about Mr. Rogers. She loved acting, but she felt called to entrepreneurship. She was so inspired by the Expo she went home and began perfecting some of her recipes for healthy ice pops. This would mark the beginning of her startup career and entice me back into the world of startups. Our adventure in this together didn't exactly turn out as we had planned.

 **A friend may have a great idea for a business. Maybe she needs someone to help her get started. Maybe that someone is you. These days new businesses can start**

up with one or two people, followed by a marketing or product person (or both), a tech person (if needed), and a board of advisors and/or mentors. Sometimes it's great to have a partner who is also a friend to share the burden, but as you'll see in a later chapter, friends, and even founders, sometimes get sidelined when the money comes in.

# Chapter 13
## Freelance Fun

I've freelanced several times for my mentor, Jack, who is 10 years younger than I am. He may have been suspiciously and conveniently ready to step into my job the day I left Larry King (we joke about that today), but he's been loyal and extremely supportive of my freelance career since then. He's hired me to work for him in four of his companies because we trust each other and enjoy working together.

Long before we were both "over 50," in 1986, I'd left *CBS Morning News* to spend a few months backpacking in Asia with Doug, the year before we got married. In the Philippines, we were staying at the Manila Hotel while President Marcos was planning his exit, after the People Power Revolution challenged his third term in office.

CBS had set up a temporary bureau in the hotel, and we checked their hazard maps before heading out for our various sightseeing trips. It was pre-Internet, so we were working with paper maps, news, and guidance from local "fixers" to stay out of trouble. This was a great benefit of belonging to the global clan of network TV journalists.

A few days into our journey around the Philippines, from Banaue to Boracay to the beaches of Cebu, Doug and I went out for breakfast at a beach cafe. In place of the day's menu, the chalkboard read:

"ALL INTERNATIONAL FLIGHTS CANCELLED UNTIL FURTHER NOTICE."

Nothing like being stuck at a resort in a beautiful foreign country during a peaceful revolution. Marcos was flown to Guam on a US military plane a few days later, and there was a growing sense of optimism among the people we met as we continued of our journey.

When we flew back to the US my old friend and mentor, Jack, had just been hired to produce Charlie Rose's new late-night show *Nightwatch,* on CBS. He hired me to run the booking department. A few months after I started that job, I was offered the producer position at *Face the Nation.*

Then, after two years of getting up at 4:30 every Sunday morning for *Face the Nation,* I moved to the assignment desk. Now I was back on a daily deadline, sending crews out to cover each day's news. The slow pace of a Sunday show gave way to breaking news, day and night.

In 1988, CBS went through a round of extensive layoffs. It was a gut punch to the Washington bureau. Legendary reporters who had dodged bullets covering the Vietnam War with Dan Rather were forced into early retirement. One of those reporters was Ike Pappas.

Ike wasted no time after his dismissal to start his own production company in the building next door to CBS, where the BBC, NHK, Agence France-Press, and other foreign news organizations all had offices. I left my job to freelance for Ike because he was a lot of fun to work with, and I was burned out on the news grind after six years off and on at CBS.

**"Fun" is a perfectly legitimate reason to start something new. If you're burned out, maybe it's time to recalibrate your thinking about how you want to spend your waking hours. Stop squatting with your spurs on. Stand up, man up, and take a ride on that bucking bronco. Yeehaw!**

The Democratic National Committee hired us to produce a daily talk show backstage at their convention in Atlanta. This was 1988, when Bill Clinton gave a speech so long that when he finally said "in conclusion" the delegates cheered.

I had never been on the floor of a political convention: It was cacophonous. A ComicCon for political geeks. My days were a hodgepodge of nonstop networking, sweet-talking, and confirming commitments from guests for that night's backstage show. My only memories from the convention floor were how hot and noisy it was, how crazy some of the delegates dressed and acted, and Bill Clinton's endless speech.

Our nights out on the town were star-studded events with celebrities, wannabes, and the ever-present, pesky paparazzi. Ike had invited his friend, film director Paul Mazursky, to join us on the convention floor and for the after-parties with stars like Meg Ryan, Judd Nelson, Mike Farrell, Lily Tomlin, Sarah Jessica Parker, and Tom Hayden, who was there as a delegate for Michael Dukakis. I confess we partied a lot harder than we worked that week.

After the convention, my next freelance gig was with another media company with offices in Ike's building. I was hired as the American producer for TV-am's *Good Morning Britain*, a popular morning chat show on ITV, based in London. The bureau chief, Chris Stocking, asked me to produce "strands," or series on life in the US.

David Foster and Anthony Dworkin were TV-am's US-based reporters. David was a proper Englishman with thick graying hair, a lovely family, and a bawdy sense of humor; Anthony was a very intelligent and shy American with a law degree. They were both entertaining travel companions. The series we produced were engaging and radically different from anything you'd see on US TV. It was fascinating to observe my home country through the eyes of a visitor, to discover what they found most interesting and newsworthy.

David wanted to do a series on our criminal justice system. Like many English people, he was appalled by the number of Americans in jails and prisons. He wanted to do our first story in a maximum-security unit. I set up interviews at Marion penitentiary in Illinois, then a "supermax" federal prison where the inmates were in "permanent lockdown" and only allowed out of their cells for one hour a day. When I'd worked in the Texas Legislature, my boss was on the prison reform committee and I had visited inmates on death row at Huntsville. I was somewhat prepared, but still a little nervous about being in a place where two guards had been murdered by inmates, members of the Aryan Brotherhood.

Our crew also spent a week in Missouri shooting stories about Branson's country music scene, and the proliferation of pot grown in the wilds of the Ozarks. Local sheriffs flew us in a helicopter over the heavily forested mountains where it was easy to spot the bright green cannabis plants down below. We landed and watched as workers chopped down plants almost as tall as a two-story building, then lit the pile of them on fire. The officers told us that the value of each plant they burned was about $25,000 back then. An exaggeration, probably, but it was impressive to see the plants growing in the wild, when they were so easily detected from the air.

After the slash-and-burn operation, we headed in a convoy to the alleged grower's house. He answered the door looking fully lit up. The dude was obviously trying to sort out why there were people with guns at his door, plus a bunch of TV gear.

Standing in front of him, smirking a bit, was a puckish reporter with a British accent. As this alleged grower was led away in handcuffs to a deputy's vehicle, David stuck a microphone in his face and asked, politely, and with what sounded like an affected trill: "Sir-r-r, you are accused of gr-r-rowing mar-r-r-ijuana in the for-r-rest. What do you have to say for yourself?"

The poor stoner looked at all of us, shook his head, and burst out laughing.

The other correspondent, Anthony Dworkin was interested in the roots of blues music. I set up a trip that would take us to Little Rock, Greenwood, and New Orleans in search of the oldest, baddest bluesmen and women still performing, and they played for us and told us stories about their musical idols. I couldn't believe I was getting paid to do this. These "strands" aired in two-minute segments each morning for a week. We had so much great footage we could have produced a wonderful music documentary, and I wish we had.

**Why should I have all the fun? Have you ever considered starting over as a journalist? If you don't have time for journalism school, why not become a "citizen journalist" and take your cellphone camera to the streets? Digital media and social media have made it easier than ever to become a "thought leader" and to try on the role of a reporter. You don't have to go journalism school. If you can get yourself hired at a news organization as an intern or a production assistant, you can learn on the job.**

In December 1988, TV-am sent me to Cuba to advance Mikhail Gorbachev's visit to the island. The soon-to-be president of Russia was reportedly planning a difficult meeting with Fidel Castro, who criticized his support of openness (glasnost) and restructuring (perestroika). Gorbachev wanted Castro to help him spread his brand of "better for you" communism in Central America. Castro needed Russia to continue their oil and sugar subsidies, and they both needed a détente.

TV-am in those days had a culture of lavish spending and frivolity. *The Guardian* called it "Snap, Crackle, and Pap." Our acting bureau chief in Havana had a fat checkbook and he wasn't afraid to use it. He furnished our penthouse suites at the Hotel Habana Libre with a mounted bull's head (just like the ones in Hemingway's favorite bar, Bodeguita del Medio), a Christmas tree, a plastic swimming pool filled with water, rubber ducks, and lots of other toys. It was an obscene display of excess capital in a country where most locals couldn't afford meat with their dinners. We partied hard, but we did what we came to do, and produced some informative and provocative stories.

We shot footage of the tattered costumes on the dancers at

the Tropicana and the lack of products in the dollar stores. We interviewed people about how they made ends meet day to day. Our minders and drivers kept tabs on us day and night, even as we all watched Castro deliver an electrifying speech with no notes—for four hours. Not even a bathroom break.

Communicating messages in simple, emotional language—telling them what they wanted to hear—was his gift as an orator. I remember he invited a young girl on stage with him to read a lengthy poem. He stood by her at the podium, stroking his beard, watching her with pride in his eyes, as if she were his own granddaughter. It was compelling television, and it helped us understand how Fidel could be both reviled and beloved. It was memorable, if chilling.

Gorbachev, who was in New York while we were in Havana, had to cut his trip short and fly back to Moscow to deal with the 1988 earthquake in Armenia. Since he never made it to Cuba, our two-week advance reporting trip was a bit of a bust. We donated all the toys and decorations to the hotel workers, and to our drivers and local fixers, before we headed back to Miami in our chartered jet. To my knowledge, the bureau chief never got in trouble for what we spent on that trip, and we all came back with suntans and great memories.

**What's your responsibility to your employer, partner or your team, vendors, or customers? Are you spending money for good reasons? Or showing off? When you're using other people's money, hold yourself accountable. Even if we got away with it, because of a laid-back corporate culture, you may not.**

After almost a year at TV-am, I got a contract with the National Space Society in Washington, DC. The executive director, Lori Garver, wanted to set up a hotline so kids in classrooms could send questions to the astronauts and hear their answers live. This was revolutionary and technologically challenging at the time. We set up an 800 number that any teacher in the country could access. Working with the Houston Space Flight Center, we all made it work.

Astronauts don't have a lot of free time. Those freewheeling, fun moments you see in news clips are rare. Every second of an astronaut's day is planned and directed by people who don't wear space suits—the men and women of mission control. But for this project the astronauts managed to find time to talk to students for the National Space Society, and the NSS accomplished its mission. This program generated new membership for the organization, and it raised their profile. Lori went on to fill the number two position at NASA in the Obama administration.

The NSS contract rekindled my childhood interest in human space exploration. So in 1989, I formed a production company (hey, another startup!) with a freelance producer I had met at TV-am, Beth Worth. We called it Worthwhile Productions.

There are companies that charge tens of thousands of dollars to name products and new businesses. It's an art, and a science. You can do it on your own, just try to own all the relevant urls and social channels. Work a benefit into the name if you can. Messaging around your company and products should emphasize benefits over features. Not "what we do" but "how you'll benefit from what we do."

We put together a plan to write, produce, and direct a one-hour documentary celebrating the 30th anniversary of the Apollo 11 moon landing. We called it *From Apollo to the Stars*. Neither of us had ever worked on a documentary before. But we thought, how hard could it be? We know TV!

NSS's Lori Garver introduced us to one of her board members, Gene Roddenberry, the creator of *Star Trek*. Gene agreed to serve as executive producer of the film, and we couldn't have had a better story adviser or high-profile name to add to our fundraising letters. But he had no documentary credits, and he knew we didn't. We were all working outside our comfort zones. Gene worked closely with us and believed in us, but he told us that raising the money was our job. He could have easily financed the entire production but he wanted us to learn how to do it on our own.

Our budget was $250,000.

We raised $125,000 in about eight weeks by phone, fax, and a few personal visits. We targeted companies that might want to be associated with Roddenberry, or with the lunar landing anniversary.

**Are you raising money for your startup? Investors want to invest: They're looking for opportunities. Even though there are far fewer investors than opportunities, it's not a zero sum game. Good companies and entrepreneurs will always find funding one way or another. Some investors like to keep their money in the same sector, like cannabis or software, or companies that have a social impact. Others like a variety. You don't have to go around hat in hand. It's all about matching what you're**

**building to their interests and motivations. Make them believe in you, and they just might open their wallet.**

One of the most shocking fundraising meetings we had for this project was with Rockwell, where a senior marketing executive questioned us about our basic thesis.

"I don't know," he said. "Maybe we've learned all we can learn from space, and maybe we need to come back and focus on more important things here on Earth." We couldn't believe we were hearing this at an aerospace firm. He didn't write us a check, and we moved on.

Other US companies largely ignored us, too, so we ended up raising most of the money overseas. Shimizu, a Japanese engineering firm with designs for a space hotel, and a Japanese pharma company gave us some funding, as did Aerospatiale in France. We also got funding from Intelsat, which hosted our premiere at their striking, futuristic headquarters in Washington, DC. Beth and I felt like we were walking the red carpet in Hollywood when we arrived that evening. We were exhausted and broke, but we were so relieved, and smiling.

Soon after our first airing on PBS we were close to a deal to sell Japan TV rights to the NHK network for $50,000. We flew to New York to finalize the deal, but when we brought lawyers in to discuss it, they changed their minds.

**Often, the US offices of overseas companies function according to customs in their own country. Are you sensitive to cultural differences in business? In your relationships? Anything can make a deal go south. Don't allow your ignorance of their business style or customs be the cause.**

During post-production Beth and I had flown from DC to LA every couple of weeks to meet with Gene in his office on the Paramount lot. He'd watch our rough cuts with a childlike enthusiasm, urging us to jettison our footage of the engineers on the ground in mission control.

"People will be living and working in space in the future. It's a fact. Show them the vision," Gene said. He later added, "In the future, no one will need space vehicles. We'll travel without them."

I had no idea what Gene was talking about. Was he a little too visionary? Years later, when I started meditating, I finally understood. Some visionaries think in centuries, not decades, and Gene was a wizard, a dreamer, and a prophet.

Making your first documentary is intimidating and exhausting but we were inspired and so honored to work with Gene, Lori, and Buzz Aldrin, the second man to walk on the moon, who had signed on as our host after Gene came on board.

Buzz had agreed to open and close the program for us, and we wanted to make sure we had the perfect location. My first husband, Doug, and I had spent our honeymoon in Portugal, and we'd stayed at a pousada in the coastal village of Sagres. It's where Prince Henry the Navigator had his sailing school. Ships were launched from this southwestern tip of Europe to explore new worlds and go "where no man has gone before." Beth and I thought Sagres would be an ideal spot to set the scene and close the program.

We flew Buzz and his wife, Lois, to Portugal for a day of rehearsals and two shoot days. We had prepared cue cards, but it was so windy Buzz couldn't read them. I begged him to memorize his lines for the opening, at least. Instead, in the evenings at dinner, he showed us his ideas for a mission to Mars, drawing the trajectories on the back of his napkin.

Buzz had no interest in reliving his past. He was focused on the future of the civil space program and that, plus a few glasses of red wine interfered with our plans to get him ready for the next day's shoot. So, like all documentary producers faced with an insurmountable challenge, we decided to wing it, and pray the TV production gods would save us.

For the closing scene, I persuaded the Portuguese Navy to take us up in a helicopter to get an aerial shot of the sailing school, free of charge. *Muito obrigada*, Portugal.

We finished the documentary in four months, barely covering our hard costs. To make our airdate, we ran two edit bays around the clock for weeks and nearly killed ourselves doing it. We managed to get the documentary on PBS, and we beat *NOVA* in the ratings in several big markets.

It took us two years of international sales just to break even. It was kind of exciting, though, to see a cassette of the Italian version in a shop window in Rome when I was shooting a TV documentary there two years later.

 **When you're doing something you've never done before, you're bound to make mistakes. It's OK. Allow yourself to be a beginner and give it your best shot. One lesson from our documentary experience: Always ask for a discount, or a freebie. Sometimes it works!**

During those freelance years, a producer for a syndicated show called *Travel and Adventure* reached out to me. She needed a field producer to go overseas with three reporters and three crews to shoot their next season of travel shows. How could I refuse?

**OPM. If you can get other people to fund your project, your company, your travel, do it! Other People's Money is the best kind of money there is, especially if you're taking on other risks: your time, your reputation, your relationships, your career. You may be tempted to max out your credit cards or take a second mortgage to finance your idea. Don't go crazy. That's what banks, family and friends, and investors are for.**

Our job was to go into a city, find the fun things to do, and build a half-hour show around them. We would shoot in Barcelona, Sevilla, Madrid and Toledo, Cancun, Jamaica, and on a cruise ship, among other locations. It was one of the best freelance contracts I've ever had, but there was a catch. The venture capitalists who owned the show had never been in television before and we never knew when or whether we would all get paid. We were on the road having a blast, eating well, controlling our own schedules, but we were checking our bank accounts back home. Sometimes the bosses delayed paying us for a few weeks. My job was to prevent a walkout while we were overseas. Eventually we all got paid, but the show was cancelled after that season.

The most vivid memories of those trips were transportation-related. One night I was driving down a narrow alley in a small town outside of Sevilla, Spain. There was a festival in the main plaza, and I had one of the show's hosts with me. People kept pointing and telling us to turn around as we headed down a small, cobblestone back street, but I ignored them. It's a good thing we had a sunroof because we got stuck. The street was so narrow people opened their doors and couldn't walk outside to go to the festival because our car was in the way. I had to have a local man climb in through the sunroof and take control. He slowly backed it up to an intersection so we could open the doors, get in, and drive away.

**Starting down a new path can be perilous. But when things go wrong, there's always a way out. And you'll have another good story to tell.**

The other vehicle mishap occurred in Barcelona. I'd maneuvered our eight-passenger rental van down three levels of an underground garage easily, *sin problemas*. But when I tried to come back up the ramp to the exit, I could hear the roof scraping against the ramp above. Cars were stuck behind us, but they weren't honking their horns, yet. Some local genius urged us to load up the van with as many people as possible, then let some air out of the tires. It worked. We rolled out onto the street, got some emergency air, and raced for the airport to fly back to Madrid. Gracias, Hertz, for not charging us for the damage to the roof!

**Do you know what you don't know? Fortunately, we live in a time when we can have an extra brain in our hands at all times, and we can find information quickly. Smartphones are great. But knowledge? Wisdom? Experience? You won't find those on Google. There's no shame in asking for help. Pick the brains of people who've been down your path before. Listen to the locals—they're the experts. It will save you time, money, and stress.**

# Chapter 14
# Sex, Scandal, and the Library of Congress

Writing a memoir is like having a near death experience. Your life flashes before you—scenes from a movie. You begin to recognize patterns in your trials and errors, resurrect memories of the people who've helped and hurt you, and recognize that every chance you took, or didn't take, somehow pitched you forward to your current life and career.

December 1987. My former NBC colleague and current bestie, Shelley Ross, hired me to research illustrations for her book *Fall from Grace: Sex, Scandal and Corruption in American Politics from 1702 to the Present.* This juicy assignment sent me deep into the collections of the Library of Congress, the oldest federal cultural institution in the United States.

I read George Washington's affectionate letters to his neighbor and possible paramour, Sally Fairfax. I saw portraits of Thomas Jefferson's neighbor and probable lover, Maria Cosway. And I learned about the New York governor general, Lord Cornbury, whose political enemies claimed he wore a velvet dress to public events, in honor of Queen Victoria.

It was a fascinating project, and it sparked my interest in working full-time in this stimulating academic environment—the most under-appreciated government entity in Washington, in my opinion.

One day as I was walking through one of the Library's tunnels on the way to the print shop, I stopped in front of the jobs board. There was a posting for a newly created position: Director, Global Library Project. The GLP was a new public-private partnership between the Library and a Denver-based cable TV company, Jones Intercable. The founder, Glenn Jones, had written a fat check to help the Library launch this initiative.

GLP's mission: Go into the Library's collections, find the hidden gems, and make TV documentaries about them. This had to be the only government job in the world as exciting as the position one of my brothers has, dealing with TV and film production. I applied and went through several rounds of interviews, plus an FBI background check. I got the job.

Starting up something that came with a decent salary and full benefits, with the freedom to create my own content, was glorious. I felt like a shopaholic at a sample sale. So many treasures, so little time. If Doug and I hadn't moved to Korea, I never would have left.

My bosses were the Librarian of Congress, Dr. James Billington; Glenn Jones, (the man with the checkbook); and John Y. Cole, the head of Cultural Affairs and creator of the Center for the Book. Three intellectuals and a lady. They were my "brain trust" and all of them were supportive bosses and helpful advisors. This was definitely a dream job for someone like me.

I developed two series of one-hour documentaries for TV: one about the Library's "treasures" and the other about the fundamental role of libraries in a democracy. The stories we uncovered were fascinating. With continued funding we could have kept on producing documentaries for decades. In all, we produced 23 shows that aired on Glenn's cable network, some aired on the Discovery Channel, and others were sold internationally.

The Library of Congress describes itself as the world's largest library. It preserves and protects more than 100 million items. Some 70 percent of the collections are in a language other than English. They have 5,000 flutes in the Dayton Flute Collection, five million maps, Stradivarius and Guarneri violins, posters, wax cylinder recordings, illuminated manuscripts, and more. It's an intellectual royal palace filled with precious jewels for a curious mind.

Thomas Jefferson's personal library was foundational to the Library's history, so I decided to do the first program about him. I went deep into the stacks and surveyed the shelves that held his books. Some were cookbooks he had bought during his trips to France. I pulled one off the shelf and found a recipe for ice cream.

I took the recipe to the chef at the Boar's Head Inn in Charlottesville, Virginia, and asked him to prepare it on camera, Food Network style. Then we went to Monticello and interviewed one of the docents about Jefferson's herb garden. The rest of the film explored how Jefferson influenced the newly minted "American" culture through his writing; his interest in other languages, science, and history; his reading habits; and his keen intellect. It wasn't a complete portrait, because I knew the Library wouldn't want us to dig too deeply into his past. This wasn't *Fall from Grace*. Hagiography over controversy. Though Glenn Jones provided some of the funding, the rest came from the Library's Cultural Affairs division budget, and they had to be careful not to create a stir with the overseers across the street. The Library of Congress depends on politicians for its funding, so there's no appetite for making waves by hosting controversial exhibits or putting out documentaries that will provoke people to write to their elected representatives.

The Rare Books collection at the Library holds the "dispatch bag" (a briefcase for maps and messages) that belonged to Christopher Columbus, another prominent person whose reputation has been reassessed in recent years.

For the Sesquicentennial of Columbus's 1492 voyage, I hired a Columbus historian to join us aboard a small ship that retraced one of the explorer's many routes through the Bahamas. For another segment of this documentary, I brought two experts together to conjure some highbrow magic. The former Librarian of Congress, Daniel Boorstin, had written *The Discoverers: A History of Man's Search to Know His World and Himself.* Philip Glass had composed the music for the new Columbus opera, *The Voyage*. I recorded the two of them interviewing each other about the mindset of a discoverer, and the joys and perils of exploration.

It was inspiring to watch these two virtuosos who had never met ask each other questions no professional interviewer would have thought of, and the answers were surprising, enlightening, and profound. Editing their hour-long discussion down to 10 minutes was challenging.

**Serendipity. When it happens to you, notice it, and don't hesitate to act. If I hadn't stopped in front of that jobs board, then applied for that job, then followed up relentlessly until they hired me, I never would have had these career-defining experiences. Train yourself to see the world they way artists do, with open eyes, an open mind, and attention to the things others overlook. Opportunities are as elusive as butterflies. And good fortune comes to those who summon it. Try writing and saying what you want and then take action in that direction. Watch what happens.**

The Library's Rare Books collection also safeguards the personal scrapbooks of magician Harry Houdini. I sent a producer to Niagara Falls to the Houdini Magical Hall of Fame (which was later destroyed in a fire) to shoot a demonstration of some of Houdini's magic props. This producer also interviewed James Randi, who revealed some of Houdini's secrets. Buzzkill, I know, but it was entertaining.

For the series on libraries and democracy, I sent a crew and producer to check the conditions in two of the national libraries of the FSU, the Former Soviet Union. The Soviet Union had collapsed in 1991, and the preservation of their cultural heritage was at stake. The crew returned to Washington with heartbreaking images of broken windows, moldy books, and pigeons pooping on some priceless manuscripts in Slovakia. We later learned that our inquiries and filming prompted the government to fix the windows and eventually fund renovations for the national library in Bratislava.

The Vatican Library was preparing to send some its treasures to the Library of Congress for an exhibition. Many of these items had never been seen outside Vatican City. I wanted to produce a film to preview the exhibit, so I traveled to Rome, and hired a local TV crew, with a cameraman I had found through my old connections at CBS.

Wearing fresh white gloves to protect these original documents, I held Henry the VIII's letters to Anne Boleyn, Ptolemy's *Geographia*, and many, many other fragile documents and books. I was breathless as I handled these priceless historical treasures.

One day, a Vatican librarian took me into an inner sanctum, where he showed me a book at least eight feet tall, gilt-edged, leather-bound, and full of hand-painted musical notes. It was an old choir book. I imagined a choir standing in front of it in a semi-circle, with enormous candelabras on each side, following the musical notations in the flickering candlelight of a vast European cathedral. The book was so large it took two people to carefully turn the pages.

If I were single at the time, I would have happily spent the rest of my working life at Library of Congress. It may be a bureaucratic government institution that answers to 535 politicians, but it was my happy place. That job provided me with some of the most thrilling and memorable experiences of my career.

I didn't think things could get any better, but they did, eventually. First, things had to get worse.

**What can you do to create your own good fortune if you're not one of the lucky few? As Angela Davis said, "I am no longer accepting the things I cannot change. I am changing the things I cannot accept." She was referring to social justice, but the same message could be applied**

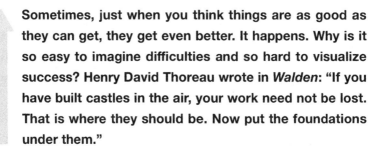

**to startups. Start something up. Work part time on a side gig and build it into a business. Volunteer, so you'll meet others with your same interests. Learn a new skill. *Audentes fortuna Iuvat*. Fortune favors the bold.**

My second husband, Don, used to say, "Don't give it a kinohara" whenever I got excited about something. It's a Yiddish/Hebrew expression meaning, "Knock on wood," or "Don't get too comfortable…you never know what could happen." Optimist-me was never on board with that philosophy. I love getting excited about things, even if it means I'll be disappointed sometimes. I can deal with that.

**Sometimes, just when you think things are as good as they can get, they get even better. It happens. Why is it so easy to imagine difficulties and so hard to visualize success? Henry David Thoreau wrote in *Walden*: "If you have built castles in the air, your work need not be lost. That is where they should be. Now put the foundations under them."**

# Chapter 15
# Nobody Knows Anything, in Politics or in Marketing

After we moved back to California in 2002, my husband, Don, the political consultant, met with some of his former competitors to solicit new business. These were Democratic political operatives he had sometimes defeated in senate and gubernatorial campaigns all over the US. They knew him and admired his work.

But political consultants are a curious bunch. You pick your side of the fence, and you're stuck for the rest of your life. As UT Football coaching legend Darrel Royal said, you've got to "dance with who brung ya." Dance with your party, or die, politically.

The Republican consultants behind the Lincoln Project, a digital content company dedicated to defeating President Trump in 2020, admitted in TV interviews they had sealed their fate with their party by going after one of their own. But don't waste your tears on political consultants. They always land on their feet, even when their own Project gets burned by a scandal. They'll be fine.

In his reinvention of self, Don challenged that paradigm. He created ads for Democratic Representatives Jane Harman and Grace Napolitano, candidates he had solicited on his own. He also wrote and directed issue advocacy media for corporate and nonprofit clients in Southern California, Sacramento, and Washington, DC.

**Knowing how to sell is everything. Always be your authentic self when you're selling your services or your company. Take an improv class. Improv teaches you how to think fast, you'll meet new people from all walks of life, and you'll have a blast. Guaranteed.**

Now that we were back on the West Coast I was hired by the infomercial division of the global ad agency EuroRSCG (now Havas). I produced a fundraising infomercial for St. Jude Children's Hospital that targeted the US Hispanic market—in Spanish.

Once I became proficient in Spanish, almost as fluent as a native speaker, the ability to read and speak it has never gone away. Total immersion in my teens seemed to tattoo the language onto my brain. I enjoy speaking Spanish on the job, and with my daughter, who had her own total immersion experience in Central and South America in 2018.

In pre-production meetings, I urged St. Jude executives to let us travel outside the walls of the hospital to demonstrate how their international programs worked in the field. Using video conferencing, St Jude's medical teams guide doctors outside the United States, especially in Central America, as they treat their young patients. If it becomes medically necessary, they transfer the patients to the hospital in Memphis for additional care.

I suggested St Jude send us to the Benjamin Bloom clinic in

San Salvador to interview some of their doctors and patients, and demonstrate how the partnership worked. They agreed. They also invited Luis Fonsi, the Puerto Rican singer, and Angelica Vale, a Mexican actress and singer, to serve as hosts for this fundraising infomercial.

Have you ever been touched by an appeal from a nonprofit helping children, animals, or older people? How about those sad puppies on the Humane Society fundraising infomercials? We created some of those while I was a producer for EuroRSCG Edge. We had to walk the fine line between drawing people in and turning them away.

**Messaging anything with just the right amount of "make me care" will give you the best chance at success. So if you're trying to get someone to buy into your idea, show them you've identified a problem, and, with their help, the problem can be solved. Show them the delta between where you are, and where you could be with their support.**

Our Spanish-language infomercial and the many versions created after I was involved have raised millions from the Spanish speaking community in the US. Richard Davies, St. Jude's own writer/producer, and Marc Kravets, EuroRSCG's direct marketer, deserve much of the credit for this phenomenal fundraising success. I'm honored to have been a small part of an effort to help raise funds for this wonderful place of hope for children with cancer.

# Chapter 16
# Fitness, Music and Enchantment

After I left EuroRSCG, I worked on an Internet startup with a small team that included Ricki Lake. Ricki was a popular daytime TV talk show host in the 1990s and early 2000s. She also starred as the "fat girl" with the sensational voice in John Waters's *Hairspray*.

Throughout her childhood, Ricki had struggled with her weight, and like most overweight kids, she was bullied and fat-shamed. As a mother of two young boys, she wanted to do something to help overweight and obese children get healthier by eating better without feeling deprived or punished. Ricki was the perfect celebrity to represent an e-commerce business that offered customized meal plans for kids that didn't feel like a punishing diet. Our Web app used an algorithm to determine the proper meal plans based on desired weight loss, preferred foods, and dietary restrictions. Childhood obesity was a hot topic in the news when we launched.

Unfortunately, this startup never got much traction. Social media was very limited back then, and it took a heavy investment in digital ads to make sites like this work. The website had a lot of traffic, but not enough of the visitors converted to meal plan subscribers.

Ricki went on to produce memorable feature documentaries with her partner, Abbie Epstein. Her talk show residuals and smart investments have given her the freedom to reinvent herself as often as she wants to. I admire her commitment to exploring important causes through her films, even if they're controversial. As they used to say at the end of her shows, "Go Ricki!"

> **Are you letting your past define you? Confine you? Ricki used the pain of her past to address her childhood problem for a new generation. Instead of a cage that keeps you trapped, limiting your choices—"I'm broke, I don't have the right education, I don't have any connections"—think of your past as your raw material, your clay. You're the potter, and from this point forward, you choose the form, the colors, the glazes, the embellishments, and accents. Reach out to people who have formed their lives in ways you admire. Pick up your clay, and start molding it.**

After the online diet startup, Beachbody hired me to develop a Spanish-language version of one of their most successful fitness infomercials. P90X, with Tony Horton, is one of the most popular home fitness programs of all time. This would be an experiment, to see if there were enough Spanish speakers who might not have bought the English language version. It worked well enough that the product was made available in Mexico as well.

I also worked on Tai Cheng, a tai chi program for athletes,

boomers, and people rehabbing after an injury. Beachbody's CEO, Carl Daikeler, loved the program so much he had his elderly dad try it. But he wondered if a tai chi infomercial would work: Most of the Beachbody programs were designed for people who wanted to sweat, lose weight, or get ripped. Carl's track record in fitness was solid, but infomercials are like movies and TV shows: You never know how the audience will respond until you test them.

The trainer, Dr. Mark Cheng, had a long history in tai chi and he's an expert in functional movement. He was enthusiastic about taking the mystery out of learning the moves so people could master them quickly and easily and he was a wonderful "cue-er," a trainer who is easy to follow. Carl was willing to give it a try.

*Tai Cheng* is an easy way to learn 18 fundamental moves of tai chi in 12 weeks. It really works. Most people think infomercial testimonials are phony, but if they're developed by respected companies like Beachbody, that's simply not true. We put 100 people through the 90-day Tai Cheng program as a test group and had some outstanding results. One woman in her 80s, with a double hip replacement, returned to her favorite sport, skiing, after she completed the *Tai Cheng* program. We filmed her coming down a black diamond slope at Mammoth Mountain. It felt wonderful to be associated with a product that allowed her, and many others, to return to their active lives.

After several changes to the product positioning and the offer, the show eventually rolled out, and was successful.

Direct response on TV has been overtaken by streaming and e-commerce. I recently mentored a Capital Factory accelerator company, Livestream.tv, that offers social shopping via livestream. QVC for the space age. In their first one-hour test, for Renault's release of their first electric car, the global audience purchased a car every... I can't tell you, it's a trade secret. Let's just say the sales were very impressive, and the founders told me Renault renewed their contract.

The TV shopping audience in general is in decline now that millions have cancelled their cable service and migrated to mobile and online shopping. Infomercial companies like Beachbody, Guthy Renker, and others, with their plush offices and high overhead, have managed to survive this sea change, and I have no doubt they will retain their stature as two of the best direct response companies in fitness, wellness, and beauty.

Beachbody is uniquely positioned for continued success because of its popular meal replacement shake, Shakeology. Anyone who completes one of their fitness programs can join their network of "coaches" who sell the shake and other fitness products, and recruit other coaches.

I got in great shape with 90 days of P90X, and I had a good fitness story ("woman over 50 hates exercise, 90 days of P90X kicks her butt and improves her self-image"). But you have to keep at it.

Are you in the best shape of your life? No? I've heard, and used, every excuse not to exercise. Working at Beachbody, where we were encouraged to use the company's beautiful gym and showers any time of day, I got over it.

 **Is it time you gave yourself the gift of fitness by taking one small step? Sign up for that class. Stream that workout. Don't take your ability to move your body for**

> **granted. If you have physical limitations, do whatever you can, but don't do nothing.**

Beachbody paid me a great salary with a generous bonus, and I reported directly to the CEO, who was a wonderful boss. It's the only company I've ever worked for that had plenty of female executives. It was refreshing to sit in a conference room full of women who were empowered to make decisions.

Unfortunately, my skills weren't a great fit for the job: too much project management. I needed to be in a more creative role with a left-brained partner or have a staff that could handle the minutiae. I don't enjoy generating charts and spreadsheets, but I'm great at finding their shortcomings. I think that's because I'm a scanner, as opposed to a driller. Assess. Obsess. Finesse. That's what I do best.

> **Have you assessed your real strengths? Not what you majored in in college, or what you've been doing in your current job, but what are you really good at? Or what you love? Look up the Japanese concept of Ikagai, which means "reason for being." There are good diagrams on the Internet that can serve as templates for your self-evaluation.**

After Beachbody, I met an Englishman named Dan Morrell who asked if I would help him with a music startup. Dan had spent several years in advertising, hanging out with famous UK recording artists whose music he used in his commercials. Even if the startup didn't work, I knew I was in for an entertaining experience. Start me up!

Based on his Facebook posts, I would say Dan has done his share of psychedelics. He must have been tripping when he came up with this big idea to use music to drive donations to a charity. Music. Donations. Charity. Kind of complicated, so keep those three words in mind.

He called his startup CHANT, and here's how it worked.

1. There are seven musical notes or tones linked to seven colors and seven causes.
2. Users choose a cause they care about (animals, water, the atmosphere, plants, etc.).
3. They find the note associated with the cause.
4. They "chant" the note into their phone and upload the audio to the cloud.
5. A well-known London DJ downloads everything. He makes beats using the voices in various combinations. The beats get released as short music tracks.
6. The tracks are offered to musicians to lay into their songs, and the publishing rights are shared with the CHANT Foundation.
7. The CHANT Foundation funds programs that support the seven cause areas, so a chanter's voice is their vote and their support for their favorite cause.

At concerts, people would wave their phones in the air with the CHANT app lit up in the color of the cause they supported so they could find each other.

CHANT was a charming, if perplexing, startup. The concept had so many moving parts, it would be challenging to pitch it to an investor. But I was so enchanted, I agreed to work for deferred compensation (plus equity) until Dan raised his first funds. I recruited a former colleague, Scott Kelly, to join us. Scott and I were promised a one percent stake in the company, if, and when it got funding.

**Are you working in a startup company, hoping to cash in on your equity? Working for equity feels more rewarding than working for a low hourly rate. Sometimes it pays off. Usually, it doesn't. Set your expectations accordingly.**

Dan found us some shared workspace in a beautiful Tuscan villa above Sunset Plaza, a fashionable dining and shopping area between Hollywood and Beverly Hills. The main house was in terrible condition when three Hollywood producers leased, furnished, and landscaped it, and converted it to a production hub/party house. They set aside a sunny room on the second floor for us while we got CHANT ready for launch.

These producers—our landlords—expected introductions to the high-net-worth Angelenos we would attract with the enCHANTed art gallery we planned to set up in the carriage house at the end of the driveway. We were going to dazzle some jaded, wealthy Angelenos with our trippy little social impact startup.

By September 2012 we had our first funder.

**Some of the best gigs you'll ever get are unpaid at first. Don't let that stop you if it feels right, and you think you'll get some good contacts out of it. Learn some new skills. Or at least have an unforgettable experience.**

One of the producers in our office introduced us to an Academy Award-winning filmmaker, and Dan talked to him about directing a feature film about CHANT. We were already "enCHANTing Hollywood," as Dan put it. Unfortunately, the filmmaker never made our movie, but we didn't take it personally. Making movies is always a moonshot: The director, the writer(s), the stars, and the financing all have to align. If it happens, it can take years. But we were in a hurry to get this project launched.

Dan persuaded a well-known Antarctic explorer and a London art dealer, among other prominent friends of his, to join our board of advisors. We had several meetings with a well-known music producer. These meetings were polite, and long, and usually ended with "We love ya" but no commitment. Again, not uncommon in Hollywood, but I'm sure industry professionals were mystified by this unconventional social venture called CHANT.

We met with top LA PR firms, ad agencies, branding agencies, and a well-known recording impresario, who tried to find a way to use CHANT in his new business with pop-up music production booths.

There was a lot of action, but no traction.

I was spellbound watching Dan maneuver around the edges of the entertainment industry. I was merely an observer at his meetings, and thought I was being taught how fundraising worked in Hollywood. Instead, I learned that you can't sell an idea with so many levers and gears and parts without an engine. We had great partnerships, but we needed a technical co-founder, and we needed to build a platform for the business. We also needed a much simpler way to tell our story, or a simpler story.

 **Are you looking for your first investor? Nobody wants to go first, do they? Nobody wants to miss out on the next big thing, either. Raising funds is more art than science.**

> **It's a question of building enthusiasm, managing expectations, and finding the right fit between your idea and an investor's interests. Yes, they want to see the numbers and the product and the plan, but they also want to believe in your ability to execute.**

Our initial CHANT investment didn't last long. But it did cover Dan's trip to Doha, Qatar, for the UN Climate Change conference of 2012. He presented CHANT to all the delegates in the general session. He held a press conference there. Great PR. He also went around with his cellphone and recorded individual delegates "chanting" for their favorite causes. Some of these videos are still up on YouTube at this writing.

Dan really understood the value of partnerships and video storytelling, which might have led to investment if only we could demonstrate how we would make a business out of it.

He and I went through the arduous process of writing an 88-page business plan for Enchanted Productions. This was the for-profit business that would fund the CHANT Foundation by securing and collecting music publishing rights. The business plan and pro forma made it look attractive, if not bulletproof.

Some well-known musicians in England had verbally agreed to use our "chanting voices" tracks in their music, but it was still unclear how the business would function day to day. The last time I went into the mansion there were leaves and dirt everywhere. The luxurious furniture had been removed, and the house was completely abandoned, a metaphor for the death of a startup, and the empty promises of Hollywood.

No matter where CHANT goes from here, the experience of working with Dan and Scott and Rose, our intern, was unforgettable. We failed to bring Dan's beautiful idea to life, but I have no regrets. I would work with Dan again any time.

Ideas like CHANT are so high-minded and so revolutionary, it might take a decade or two to catch on. If anyone is willing to invest in CHANT as a business, the sponsorships, ringtones, publishing rights and other revenue sources could pay off handsomely. I saw the numbers. The potential is there.

**Execution matters most. A Web or mobile-based company should start with a technical team, then build the soft skills. CHANT did it in reverse. Now they know. Even a beautiful, meaningful idea like CHANT has to function as a business and show some traction before an investor will consider it.**

# Chapter 17
# Starting Up and
# Starting Over, Again

In 2013, just as CHANT was winding down, my actor friend, Wendy Makkena, was ready to launch her frozen fruit and veggie pops in retail. She asked if I would help her start a food company.

An inquisitive reader and researcher, and one of the most detail-oriented and creative thinkers I've ever worked with, Wendy was a safe bet: I knew she'd spent three years in R&D, and she had the funds to support a product launch.

This is a founder who had taken her time to interview experts, foodies, and other startup founders to educate herself about food safety, manufacturing, distribution, retail, frozen food, and business in general.

This "mompreneur" was driven by passion as much as profit. She had always tried to give her daughter, Ruby, wholesome foods and snacks when she was growing up. Now she wanted to offer other parents a healthy treat for their kids, one that also happened to taste great. And it did! Everything from the mouth feel of the rocket-shaped pop to the full-flavored sweetness inside was the result of Wendy's years of experimenting in her kitchen. When we scaled up, we also added probiotics, which were expensive, but worth the investment to distinguish our products as "functional food," a hot category in retail.

> **If you're growing a CPG business, don't compromise on ingredients. It shows. Price is important, but do you want your customer to buy your product more than once? Make it taste/feel/work great! This sounds like a no-brainer, but it's amazing how many grocery products we eat and drink that don't taste as good as they could. Sometimes the original recipes are lame. Sometimes, it's just plain greed. Don't be greedy.**

Wendy had spent several years trying to recruit a former frozen food marketing and sales professional to help her launch a company. He finally agreed to come on board when I did. The three of us worked together to get boxes and samples ready for Expo West in March 2014. This annual trade show (the same one I took Wendy to a year earlier) started in 1981 with 3,000 attendees. Today it draws more than 100,000 people, with vendors sampling thousands of natural products: from skin care to pet food to supplements, food, and beverages. It's an important launch pad for startup companies: Buyers come from all over the world to discover new products.

I bought a used gelato case to display our frozen pops for buyers who might stop by for a sample. We weren't officially in business yet, but a "co-packer" (manufacturer) Wendy had discovered several years earlier agreed to produce a small run of 3,000 pops for our booth. Shipping and storing them at the Expo would have cost us a fortune so this dear man, bless him, delivered the pops to us with his own car. I can't tell you his name because the world of co-packing is a black box. Who you use as a co-packer is a trade secret.

We were nominated for most innovative new product, which helped us stand out from the dozens of other frozen treats on the show floor. About a month after the Expo, we were thrilled to get our first purchase orders from Central Market in Texas and Zupan's in Oregon. By July we were ready for an "angel" investor. (Angels usually step in after you've tapped out your friends and family and before you get venture capitalists involved.)

We hired an investment management firm to provide back-office support and strategic advice. They worked on our pro forma and helped us put our investment deck together.

> **You can raise "smart money" or "dumb money" or a combination of the two. Smart money is investment that offers additional benefits, such as industry expertise and connections that can help your company grow. Dumb money doesn't mean the investor is "dumb," it's just someone who wants to write a check and get a return on his/her investment. Always be honest with investors. Even if they took the time to look under the hood before they wrote a check, nobody likes surprises, and you could end up in court.**

Wendy's husband had dinner with a high school friend who happened to know an investor looking for an opportunity in CPG—consumer packaged goods. She introduced the investor to Wendy, and the match was made.

**When you start out looking for funding, you never know where you'll find your first investor. Check your high school yearbook! Ask around, renew old acquaintances, talk it up. Don't be shy. Everyone connected to you has a network of their own, so do the math. More people, more potential for the right fit.**

We had an excellent product, and we were generating demand for it. Now it was just a matter of getting more orders and wider distribution. In our favor, The American Masters of Taste gave us their Award of Excellence (like the *Good Housekeeping* seal of approval, but from chefs and foodies). Ruby Rockets was also one of Oprah's picks in *O, The Oprah Magazine*. *Parents* magazine included it in their top 25 packaged foods for families and *Family Circle* praised our red pop (made with strawberries, lemons beets, carrots, and sweet potatoes) as "outstanding."

With an infusion of cash, we could now fill new orders and pay ourselves a small salary. We were able to get our pops into over a thousand stores our first year in business. But retail products also need brand awareness, and a way to get customers to try and eventually buy them. We knew we would need to invest in sampling, marketing, and merchandising, and we would need a lot more funding to make that happen. We had hit a classic bump in the road.

The investor doubled down, thank goodness. He believed in the product, but the more we grew, the more other people wanted to take over and run the company. In my opinion, Wendy could have been an extraordinarily effective manager if she had also had a strong co-founder or COO by her side, but she had no prior experience in business and that always makes investors nervous.

The Board cut a deal with Wendy to compensate her for her substantial initial investment but limited her role in the company to being the face of the brand. She wasn't happy about it, but she agreed.

Can you imagine the shock of being told your services are no longer needed at a company you started? It happens. Especially when outside investment dollars are at risk.

> **Keep control of your board for as long as you can, or you may find yourself starting over. Having equity is not the same as growing the company you birthed. It hurts.**

I'll leave the details for Wendy's memoir, which I'm sure will be as juicy as a melted pop on a hot summer day. As the founder's ally, I was offered a lesser role in the company, too, but I chose to leave, keeping my vested shares.

At this writing, the company is still in business, developing new products and looking for a buyer. As a shareholder, I sure hope they do well. Food products are nearly as risky as infomercials. Even with a good market fit, they need deep pockets to compete with all the other products on the shelves.

> **Dreaming of starting a food, beverage, or another type of CPG company? There are more than 40,000 items, or SKUs (stock-keeping units), in the average grocery store. Consider creating products that are shelf stable, and start with three SKUs. The freezer case is probably the most competitive space in the store, and you need to spread out with multiple SKUs so your brand gets noticed.**

# Chapter 18
# The Idea Factory, and More Short Lessons in Entrepreneurship

There are only three times I've had to use my résumé to get a job: the Texas Legislature, *CBS News*, and the Library of Congress. The rest of my jobs and projects have come to me through cold calls and personal referrals. Word of mouth = the best marketing.

**A good network and strong references are essential to starting over. Even a short-term engagement or a temp job can give you both, if you're a rockstar. Starting over doesn't always mean wiping the slate clean, though. You can't run away from your reputation. Everything you do professionally puts you in contact with people who can either move you ahead or hinder you. Give it your all, even if it's a short-term gig. You never know where it could lead you.**

Being the age of most CEOs, and twice the age of many recruiters, applying for corporate jobs, even if I'm over-qualified is a waste of time. Not interested anyway. I have to take the advice I give my clients: Decide when, how, and with whom you are willing work your a** off. That includes the investors, advisors, and team members you bring on board. Set the bar high.

I only want to work for decent, honest people who are trying to make the world better through their products, services, or ideas. YOLO, baby.

While some people think vision and mission statements are old fashioned, they are indispensable, even for solopreneurs like me. They help inform every decision you make—what you read, where you invest, how you spend your time, who you hire, and why.

Having contracts with the childhood obesity website, the ice pop company, and CHANT were exciting adventures in startup world, but they weren't my first rodeos.

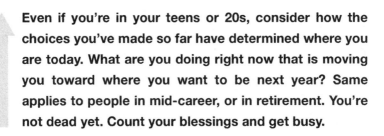

**Even if you're in your teens or 20s, consider how the choices you've made so far have determined where you are today. What are you doing right now that is moving you toward where you want to be next year? Same applies to people in mid-career, or in retirement. You're not dead yet. Count your blessings and get busy.**

In my twenties, with some down time between jobs, I launched a consulting company and called it The Idea Factory. I opened an office in downtown Washington, DC, hired a personal assistant and then....crickets.

I needed a client. I had no clue how to get one.

So I made a cold call to National Geographic Television and set up an appointment with one of the executive producers. In the meeting I said, "I'd like to produce something for you." My timing was perfect. They happened to have a small project and they were looking for someone to get it done quickly. They took a chance on me.

I hired the best and most creative editor I knew, and we wrote, produced and edited the first series of promos for *National Geographic Explorer*.

Bingo. They paid on time, but they didn't have any other projects that weren't assigned in house, so I moved on.

Next, I pitched the National Wildlife Federation on developing a radio series for their comic book character Ranger Rick. They hired me to write a treatment, a budget, and some sample episodes. My contract might have been renewed if I hadn't shown up to a meeting wearing a raccoon coat. Duh.

 **Do you know your potential client's hot buttons? Would you wear a Yankees baseball cap to interview at the Dodgers? Or drive a Chevy to pitch Mercedes on a business venture? Check yourself.**

In 1992, I met Jan Scruggs, who started the Vietnam Veterans Memorial Fund, and Sandie Fauriol, who raised the funds to get the memorial built on the national mall. They were in the final stages of planning the ceremony to commemorate the 10th anniversary of the memorial.

The VVMF had commissioned Frederick Hart who sculpted the bronze statue known as "The Three Servicemen," which would face the wall. They hired me to come up with a creative way to incorporate the wall and the statue in an official commemorative poster. The image should, they said, help unite the veterans who favored Maya Lin's original stone wall, and those who wanted a more "realistic" depiction of their experience.

The genius of Lin's important monument lies in its simplicity and timelessness. Anyone who has been there has seen how the wall casts a spell on visitors. They speak softly to each other or remain silent as they walk down the gentle slope to the center. The young architect must have known when she chose the black, polished granite that the experience of seeing your own reflection among the 58,000 names of the dead would be heartbreaking. It is especially moving when raindrops streak over the soldiers' names, like tears.

I hired Sid Smith, a photographer and Vietnam vet, to produce an image that would combine the wall and the statue, maintaining the artistic integrity of each. I wanted something iconic.

Sid spent several days observing people as they walked along the path and stopped to contemplate the wall. He decided to do something simple and unpretentious, and his final image was powerful. It was a black-and-white photo of the statue reflected in the wall itself, as if the men on the statue were reading the names of their fellow servicemen and women—as if they were standing among them.

I published 10,000 posters for the weekend's commemoration events.

Heavy rains were predicted for Saturday, so even though the posters were already printed and packaged flat, I had all of them hand-rolled, and individually wrapped in plastic, so they'd be easy to carry in the rain.

That Sunday, *The Washington Post* used a very similar photo on their front page, to illustrate a story about the weekend's events. The *Post* photographer had had the same idea.

**Imitation is flattering, so why does it bother you, so long as they're not stealing your intellectual property? They wouldn't copy you if they didn't admire your work and it validates your idea. Several people can have the same idea at the same time. It happens often in the world of startups.**

By the end of the weekend, we had only sold 1,000 posters. I took the rest home and stored them in my basement, my closets, my attic, wherever I could find room.

The next week I made a cold call to Asa Baber, a columnist at *Playboy*, to persuade him to write about Sid, the wall, and the poster. He did, and it was published a few months later. I started getting bulk orders for cases at a time. I shared the revenue with the VVMF and the photographer.

When I had a few boxes left, I reached out to a top official at the Veterans Administration. He sent me a list of all the VA hospitals around the country. I donated the rest of the posters to several VA facilities, to give away to the Vietnam veterans they served.

**Never overestimate a crowd, a consumer's appetite for your product, or the size of a rainstorm. If you're starting something new that's being launched at a special event, make sure the organizers are legit, and their estimated crowd sizes are credible. Also, adjust your plans once you check the weather forecast. You could sample ice pops on a cold, rainy day, and Ruby Rockets did, but I don't recommend it.**

# Chapter 19
# My Mom,
# the Startup Queen

My mother grew up in rural western Pennsylvania, 30 miles from the home of the notorious, shadow-seeking celebrity groundhog, Punxsutawney Phil. She was a lonely little girl, with a much older brother and sister who'd left for college when mom was in elementary school. She had some chickens, and a dog, but few friends nearby.

Mom wrote in her own (unpublished) memoir that she had always had a fertile imagination, befriending the "fairies" that inhabited the woods behind her house. She played piano, read poetry, and sang Scottish ballads with her father, who took care of her, mostly.

Her mother was devoted, but distant—a strong-willed, severe woman who always wrapped her long, braided pigtails in a crown on top of her head, secured by dozens of hairpins. It was not at all fashionable, but it was her way of hiding her long, flowing mane from everyone but her husband. It was, like her personality, austere. She was the president of the local Republican women's club, and she was a prude, but she filled their home with classical music, and had big dreams that her youngest child, my mother, was meant to fulfill.

After a dozen years of ballet, tap and modern dance lessons, and teaching at Interlochen's summer music camp in Michigan, mom applied to Juilliard when she was 17.

She was rejected.

Her mother wasn't having it. She called the admissions office and told them they were making a big mistake. Presumptuous, I know, especially for a woman. In the early 1950s American women were largely disenfranchised. Women couldn't even open a bank account without a man's signature back then. My grandma was an English teacher and a poet and an art lover, but she was no pushover. As a child she had gathered coal that fell from passing trains to sell to neighbors, so the family could eat. She was not about to give up on Juilliard, to have her daughter miss her shot at a dance career.

My grandmother's advocacy must have impressed them. The admissions officers created one additional, probationary, slot in their dance program for my mom. She would have to prove herself in the first semester at Juilliard or pack up her tutus and go home.

Mom moved into the Parnassus club on West 115th street in Manhattan, a women's boarding house across the street from Columbia University. There were writers' rooms and rehearsal rooms, an ornate salon where they held Sunday recitals, and a rooftop deck where the ladies had afternoon tea together.

On the main floor, the residents entertained their gentlemen friends in the parlor, with a chaperone. Mom was courted by a handsome law student who lived in a fraternity house around the corner.

In the middle of her second year in New York, mom found out she was pregnant, with me. She withdrew from Juilliard, and dad left Columbia Law School so they could move in with his parents in Virginia. Dad immediately enrolled at TC Williams Law School and worked nights as a clerk in a convenience store. It must have been quite a shock for both of my parents, but especially for mom since it meant the end of her dance career.

After I was born, we moved to a tiny apartment in the Fan District of Richmond not far from my grandparents' home in Spotswood Park. My nana helped take care of me: Mom was only 19 when I was born, and since she had no younger siblings, she had no idea how to take care of a baby.

Even though her feet used to bleed sometimes from dancing in toe shoes, she loved ballet—and modern dance—and most of all, she loved performing in front of an audience. She told me later she lamented her lost opportunity to dance with the New York City ballet company. Much later in life, she would return to the stage in a very different, yet fulfilling, role.

Mom must have missed her life in the big city as she raised four kids in a remote, conservative Southern town. We had moved to this rural, tobacco growing area after my dad took the bar exam and bought a law practice from an attorney who wanted to retire. When we were young and had babysitters, mom worked part time in his office as his legal secretary. She knew nothing about the law: My dad had to train her.

At 26, now with four kids, she got a second part-time job: teaching music at the local elementary school. By the time I was in high school she needed an escape from parenting all of us, so she started performing in local and regional theater. She was thrilled to be back in front of the floodlights.

In 1976 my parents divorced, and mom moved to Richmond to work for a law firm. A few years later, she moved to Denver, at the invitation of a new boyfriend. Though the relationship didn't work out, she fell in love with Colorado and never left.

> **If you just got laid off, or divorced, have you considered a move? New city, fresh start. If the expense of moving all your stuff is stopping you, sell it. It will help you make the transition, too. Nothing like a nice new sofa to mark the beginning of the rest of your life. Moving is expensive, but the less you accumulate, the less you have to deal with when inevitable changes occur. Get rid of anything that's not deeply personal or sentimental.**

At 60, my mother was more determined than ever to raise her profile. She somehow persuaded Big Fish, a Denver talent agency, to take her on as a client. They sent her to acting classes, and she sparkled. She booked so many commercials and indie films, my actor friends in LA and New York wanted to know her formula for success. "Two facelifts, four eye jobs, and a great attitude," was her reply.

She was an extra in the movie *Dumb and Dumber* and has had major roles in dozens of indie films, training videos, and local and regional commercials. Even today, at 87, she still gets bookings.

Mom is now married to a retired economics professor. Starting over for her meant reading the classics, hiking, and camping with her outdoorsy husband and learning to go through customs. They have lived and traveled all over the world since they met.

Mom had only used her passport once before she was 50. Now she's lived in Bulgaria, Japan, and Korea, and traveled in 75 other countries, including all the "stans" except Afghanistan.

At 80, she took a one-week trip down the Amazon, and a year later cruised through the Panama Canal. She went to Italy last year and plans to go back to Europe this Fall for the 30th anniversary of the American University in Bulgaria, where her husband taught economics and she freelanced as a theater, music, and ESL teacher. Mom frequently says she wants to die in a revolution. If she keeps traveling to some of the places she favors, she's tempting fate.

She started Ellen's Bed and Breakfast in her Victorian home in Longmont, Colorado, and managed it successfully for 25 years. Whenever she felt like traveling, she'd just stop taking bookings for a while. Not many entrepreneurs can start and stop their businesses that easily, but she was not about to let her business get in the way of her adventures.

I begged her to upgrade the sheets and buy softer pillows and thicker towels, but she was the mistress of pinching pennies, and somehow it didn't affect her business or her reviews. She never advertised, and always had more business than she could handle. If I planned to visit, she wouldn't save the main guest room for me until she was sure she didn't have a paying guest who wanted it. If she did, I'd get one of the bunk beds in the other bedroom. Once she'd rented the bunkroom, too, and I had to sleep on the floor in her room.

Though she's traveled widely, my mother is proud of her frugal lifestyle at home. Until recently she drove a Subaru with 250,000 miles on it. She buys almost all her clothes in thrift stores. I've inherited her extreme aversion to paying retail, which I consider another marketable skill. I'm great at finding good deals for clients.

> **Even after retirement, even in your 70s and 80s, if you are called to start a new business, or a new career, there's nothing stopping you. You may have other issues, but you're not too old. So long as you're healthy, starting something in your 70s and 80s can enrich your life, and may even provide some extra income.**

My mother and her husband have paid their mortgage, and they have a comfortable pension, plus good investments, but she's as restless as ever. She launched a startup business called the "Silver Circuit," a live entertainment show for seniors in assisted living and retirement communities. Mom and her acting partner perform songs and one-act plays for the older residents all around central Colorado. One of their original plays, *Senior Moments*, is witty and bawdy and the residents who aren't chitchatting or nodding off seem to enjoy it. They're a tough audience, but mom doesn't mind. She's back in the limelight.

The signs these days point toward another generation of entrepreneurs in the family. My daughter has no desire to work for "the man." And the moxie, creativity, and invincible spirit she inherited from her grandmother are traits she'll need to succeed in whatever she chooses to do.

# Chapter 20
# Good Clients, Bad Babysitter: The Juggling Act Continues

More than 10 years after I edited the prostate health book for Dr. Katz, I felt called to write and edit again. I had written travel articles for the *Los Angeles Times* and profiles for *The Washington Post, E–The Environmental Magazine, Healthy Living, Natural Health Retailer,* and *Yoga Business Journal.* I felt I now had enough credentials to pitch another writing or editing project, or start writing my own book.

Then I heard someone interviewed on a podcast who rocked my world: I wanted to help him tell his sensational life story. It would mean putting my own book on hold, but I was willing to do that if I was destined to edit his book first.

Rich Roll, an ultra-marathoner who used to struggle with addiction, did a great interview with Khalil Rafiti that lasted almost two hours. I was busy that day but I couldn't bring myself to turn it off, so I kept it on in the car between my meetings. I was so drawn to Khalil's incredible life story, that I found his phone number and called him the next day. He agreed to meet me the following week at a juice bar he and his girlfriend had started in Malibu, SunLife Organics.

 **Sometimes your media diet leads you to your best opportunities. Download those podcasts! Set aside at least an hour a day to scan for articles or posts that could help you develop business.**

The son of Lebanese and Polish immigrants, Khalil was raised in Detroit. For years his father physically and sexually abused him. His simmering rage led to drugs, alcohol, jail, and later a life around celebrities who drank heavily and always had drugs around. It took many years, but he finally hit rock bottom. Though he's not religious, he prayed for help after attempting suicide, and somehow took the first steps to turn his life around. He worked at a rehab facility in Malibu where he fed and nourished the bodies and souls of his "guests," who loved his healthy, delicious, signature smoothies.

Khalil told me he would love to finish writing the memoir he'd mentioned on the podcast, but his juice bar business, built on the recipes for juices and smoothies he used to make at the rehab center, had taken off and he was just too busy. I'm glad we met, though, because we clicked right away. I sense we'll do something together in the future.

Six years later, I had breakfast in Austin with Wes Hurt, the founder of Clean Cause, a sparkling yerba mate beverage company that donates 50 percent of its profits to scholarships for people in recovery. I mentioned Khalil's story to Wes and he said they had already been in touch. I was thrilled that these two entrepreneurs in recovery were on each other's radar, and both are using their businesses to help others struggling with a problem they've shared.

Khalil eventually found time to publish a memoir in 2015, and another in 2020. I highly recommend *I Forgot to Die*, and his newest book, *Remembering to Live*, for anyone considering a fresh start.

> Every new project is a chance to reinvent yourself. Books, films, political campaigns, startup companies, they are all new apparel we can try on to see if they're a good fit. We don't know how many days or years we have left to leave the world a better place. Sometimes it's not your own reinvention but lifting others through their projects that will make the biggest impact. Use your time wisely. As my conscious comrade, LA breathwork guru Bryan Ellis asks, "Are you a victim? Or a vessel?" Be a vessel.

Margaret, my daughter, was a regular customer at SunLife, and when I'd told her about Khalil's life story, she encouraged me to help him. Over the years she has drawn some incredible people into my life. I don't know what I would have done without Lisett and Jaime Lacayo, our Nicaraguan nanny and her husband, who had patiently taught me how to care for a newborn. Their own daughters, Olga and Silvia, cared for Margaret as if she were their own baby sister. She still considers them all her "second family."

Margaret has also attracted some quirky and in one case, troubled babysitters. There was the young actress who was extremely creative and "crafty" and told wonderfully imaginative bedtime stories: a South African Mary Poppins. One afternoon just as we were getting ready to leave for the theater, she called to say she couldn't come to work that day: She had done too many drugs the night before.

We were living on Rambla Pacifico in Malibu, near the top of Las Flores Canyon Road, a windy, dangerous drive, even in good weather. I was too gob-smacked to ask her if she had ever been high while driving our daughter up and down that road, but Margaret was safe. We were all sad that we had to let that nanny go.

Then there was Maesyn. I met Maesyn when she was waiting tables at the Inn of the Seventh Ray in Topanga. When she told me she played the violin, I asked if she would give Margaret some lessons.

Maesyn spent a year with us off and on. She imbued Margaret with her magical, gypsy vibes, along with her devotion to music and meditation. Maesyn was a generous, loving, and positive counterweight to our constant parental harping on Margaret about cleaning her room, being on time—all the things kids with ADD have trouble doing. Yes, Margaret has this condition, too. It tends to run in families.

Maesyn always understood Margaret. They're both artists. And they're both spiritually "woke." Even though she moved to Hawaii, to Bali, and is constantly on the road, Maesyn remains an important influence in Margaret's life. As of this writing, Margaret is in her early 20s, living the #vanlife like Maesyn used to do.

**You'll never starve if you know how to play a musical instrument. Buskers often make more on the streets than musicians with paid gigs in clubs. Learn to play a tune or two, then pack a ukulele or a harmonica the next**

time you travel, even if it's just for fun. Have you always wanted to be a musician? Every accomplished musician started the same way, picking up an instrument and either taking a lesson, or teaching themselves from online videos. Maybe it's what you were destined to do.

Margaret continues to develop her own voice as a writer, and songwriter. When she was just nine years old and homeschooled, she could dictate a story to me, fully developed, start to finish, with good characters, a strong story line, and a surprise ending. As a teenager she took classes at the Songwriting School of Los Angeles, where I hope she'll stay connected and learn to write hit songs and support her mom in her old age. Today she's still writing and recording songs, even as she explores other outlets for her creativity.

Margaret is also a masterful negotiator, a skill she got from her father. It is serving her well as she navigates the world as a young woman on her own.

I could be wrong, but I don't think she'll ever work in an office. She has a strong need to be outside, and at this age a distrust of government, "the system," anything approximating rules or guidelines. Maybe her career will be even more ADD than mine.

Lucky girl.

# Chapter 21
## Taking off the Parking Brake

My dad met a gentleman at an International Lions Club convention and struck up a friendship. Through the Lions' Youth Exchange Program, I spent the summer of my 16th year living with this man's family in Spain.

My hosts owned a beautiful modern apartment in Palma de Mallorca. They spent weekends and summers at their villa in Sa Cabaneta, a small, picturesque "pueblo pequeño" in the hills above Palma. In the afternoons while the adults were taking siestas, daughter Magdalena, son Tony, and their friend Pablo and I would sit around the local bar, eating pipas (sunflower seeds) and sampling the local firewater. I was way too young to barhop, but this was a safe spot, and Spaniards know how to moderate.

My host family understood very little English: They spoke Mallorquín to each other, but they always talked to me in Spanish. I had studied it for three years and spent the previous summer in Paraguay, so I understood almost everything they said to me.

Total language immersion was a revelation. By the end of the summer, I was dreaming in Spanish and speaking like a native—of Panama. The family said my vocabulary was impressive, but my accent made me sound like a *pueblerina*, a hick, from Central America. I would spend another year in high school Spanish, then four years in college trying to make my accent go away.

Today, I enjoy doing business with startups in Spain and Latin America. With video chat and a willingness to work ungodly hours, all things international are possible. There is no reason not to open the doors wide and let the world in if you're a consultant or a knowledge worker.

> **Don't be afraid to start doing something you've never done before. Just do it. Have you thought about building a consulting practice? What's stopping you from thinking globally? Like PR firms and attorneys, when you go out on your own, try to get paid a retainer, then bill monthly. Let the client take the financial risk: Your time is your product, and you don't want to have to wait forever to get paid. Some of my clients have paid me with their credit cards so they can get frequent flier miles.**

Insecurity and loneliness once ruled my life as the bullied kid in school. I am no longer intimidated by anything. Okay, snakes. And I'm in Texas these days, where there are more snakes than horses.

Each new address, every new job or project, every reinvention of self—even getting older—is a journey to a foreign land. These changes can make you feel vulnerable and insecure, or they can build your confidence. I have chosen the latter. While I recognize my limitations, I try not to let them define me. Meditation helps, though my practice is woefully inconsistent. I know I should do it every day. That's a change I'll make after I finish the book.

**Have you made a list of your self-limiting beliefs? Are they factual? Or just a story you've been telling yourself? You can, and must, tell yourself a new story if you're making a change. Don't let your old job title or socioeconomic status weigh you down as you step into your future. The possibilities for all of us are limited only by our willingness to accept what we can't change, and change what we can.**

I once reached out on Twitter to a gentleman from the UK whose blog on grief had moved me deeply. He tweeted back that he was on his way to LA, so I offered to introduce him to a well-known person in his industry of mindfulness and meditation.

To my surprise, he took me up on it, and I put the meeting together. He was impressed. The next day he introduced me to his partner. They were thinking of moving their business to LA and wondered if I'd like to help them find office space.

Andy Puddicombe and Rich Pierson moved their headquarters here, got funded, and hired a small staff, and opened the new headquarters of Headspace. Andy, the voice of the company's meditation app, has a TED talk with more than 12 million views, and to this day they dominate the field of app-based meditation.

I love their subscription business model, their vision, and deep commitment to their mission: to help everyone overcome their fear of meditation and use it in daily life. With all the individuals, apps and companies in the "mindfulness" space, I think Headspace will be the most influential long-term. As *Wired* opined, "Headspace is helping cause a cultural shift in how we think and talk about meditation."

**Successful people do things they don't want to do, because they know they should. Like exercise. And meditation. See? It's so easy to give advice, and hard to take it from yourself. What do you do to keep yourself calm in times of transition? Starting over means stepping into the unknown. That takes faith in yourself, and in the universe, God, or whatever you believe in. Faith is everything.**

Starting a new business, building an app, solving a problem through an invention or a service—these are never easy to do. "Overnight successes" aren't built without a lot of late nights, brutally hard work, creative tension, strained relationships at home, drama, coffee, and pizza. And maybe more than a little inspiration from above, around, within.

Product Hunt, Quirky, Grommet, and crowdfunding sites like Republic are a great antidote to a daily news diet of what's wrong with the world. These organizations and many others help the brave, creative founders and inventors attract investors, partners, and global business opportunities.

A few years ago, I joined a private club called FoundersCard. They offer networking opportunities with other member entrepreneurs, plus discounts on travel, computers, and wireless service. It's been a privilege to get to know some of my fellow startup entrepreneurs in various cities. Most have a mission loftier than just making millions: They really want to change the world, as I do. FoundersCard members I've met are into everything from manufacturing sustainable stylish shoes in Peru, to coffee subscription services, to e-sports and brain games.

Through AngelList, an online marketplace for entrepreneurs

and investors, I've connected with some exceptional overseas companies. One of them, Remente, is based in Sweden, a country that encourages its entrepreneurs to think globally from the day they launch. In my experience, Swedish companies are very open to partnerships with their US counterparts, so put them on your list if you're looking for opportunities overseas.

When we first talked back in 2014, David Brudö, the Remente founder, told me that they were positioning their product as brain fitness, going beyond the gaming and mindful meditation apps here in the US. Now, they've pivoted to goal-setting and cognitive behavioral therapy. Remente's core team included a psychologist, a marketer, a growth hacker, and an engineer, and they're not much bigger today. App companies don't need large teams to be successful, just the right team members with complementary skill sets. David is a serial entrepreneur who had already built successful travel deal and nanotechnology sites. With their track record and some potential US investment, I thought this company had great potential. Unlike many app startups, they're still in business 10 years later.

Our scheduled half-hour became a nearly two-hour fishing expedition, in which David and I explored all of the interests we had in common, and tried to figure out a way to work together. In the end, I got some good business intelligence from our conversation. Sometimes that's just as valuable.

David was a serial entrepreneur. As a co-founder of a cooking subscription service in Europe, he understood the subscription business model for home delivery of fruits and vegetables. Since I had been informally advising a company in LA called Out of the Box Collective (now Narrative Food), I wanted to learn more about how this type of business worked in other countries.

**Everyone you meet—from your hairdresser to your child's teacher—has networks of their own. Start the conversation by asking about their interests first, then see if there's a way to trade favors. Even if it doesn't lead to business right away, it may get you hired months or even years later. Keep those doors open.**

Narrative Food's mission is to support their customers in the kitchen, telling the stories of where their food comes from, and different ways to use it. They connect their community to local, regenerative/organic ranchers and farmers, and encourage people to cook for their families and loved ones. Every week, the founder, Jennifer Piette, curates a glorious bounty of artisanal products, meats, desserts, fruits and vegetables, and pantry items from small to medium-sized makers and growers. The online store sells subscription bundles and individual items.

Jennifer went through a rigorous application process and audit to become a best practices "B" corp. Consumers who care about the environment, fair labor practices, and sustainability favor "B" corps, which share those values and contribute to a charity or provide some other form of social impact.

**Ethics matter. In life and in business. Startups come and go, but the startup community is small and the players rotate. Sleazy business practices are as toxic as chemical waste.**

After a decade in business Jennifer has taken on very little investment, maintaining almost total control of her company. This may have limited her growth and her social life, since she works such long hours, but she's satisfied and proud of what she has built, and so am I, on her behalf. In an interesting twist of fate, when the pandemic struck, Narrative Food's sales tripled overnight, enabling her to finally grow her team and scale the business.

I became a customer of Jennifer's several years ago, and I'm a big fan or her thoughtfully curated food and beverages. Now that I'm in Texas, I'm a loyal customer of Blue Apron, Every Plate, and Imperfect Foods, but I'll always have a fondness for those heavenly local boxes in LA.

Not every startup can be a "B" corporation, but when you see that mark on a product or company, you'll know they've made the extra effort; they're conscious capitalists. Even if you don't aspire to "B" corporation status, try to do the right thing when you start over. And vote with your wallet by supporting companies that care about the four P's: people, profits, planet, and purpose.

# Chapter 22
# Startups: The Community

In 2014, I volunteered at Silicon BeachFest, a startup conference in Santa Monica that used to be one of the best networking opportunities in the LA area for founders and investors. I had a breakfast meeting with Michael Tringe, CEO and a co-founder of the digital media training and content company, CreatorUp. He asked me to join his advisory board.

Two years later, I joined the company as a consultant, helping them assemble their creative talent pool, and working on materials for them as they sought another round of investment. The company skyrocketed in 2020, when, due to COVID-19, video production and training in video content creation was in high demand. I'm glad I kept my advisor stock options. Maybe they'll go public one day.

I met someone else at a Silicon Beach Fest who later became a colleague, and a friend.

Before the conference, I'd been curious about Wadoaah Wali, who was scheduled to appear on a panel on LGBTQ startups. I sent her a message through LinkedIn. We had a quick tea together then I followed up with an e-mail. A few weeks later she asked if we could meet again.

Over lunch at a cafe in Brentwood, Wadooah told me that the startup she'd worked for the previous year was acquired, and she had taken some time off to travel. She'd also written, directed, and produced her first documentary, *Gaze of the Beholder*, about beauty, body image, and self-acceptance. The film won awards, but now she had been offered a new opportunity, and she wanted my advice.

Wadooah had met a senior network TV executive who'd invited her to submit a scripted series for prime time. She couldn't decide if she should do that, or build her personal brand, or try another documentary project.

I referred her to CreatorUp for freelance work while she tried to decide what to do, and they hired her to train their clients in digital content strategy.

**Are you listening carefully when people talk to you, even in casual conversation? Or are you just formulating your response? Deep listening is something you owe your conversation partner and yourself. Attentive and focused listeners can help potential clients find reasons to hire them. The client's needs are not always obvious. Sometimes they're teased out in conversation, if you're paying attention.**

A few weeks after our lunch I'd signed a new client, a US network TV anchor who wanted to explore other opportunities. Her contract would be up in a couple of years, and she wanted to start looking for ways to leverage her high profile and her credibility as an internationally recognized news anchor to do something completely different. This anchorwoman is full of creative ideas. She has impeccable taste, and in my opinion, she's even more beautiful than Diane Sawyer was in her younger days.

Now you know, it's not Diane.

We began with an extended discussion of her goals, her mission, and her intended audience. She told me she had an idea for a scripted TV series, loosely based on her life. She wanted to pitch it to a network. I immediately thought of Wadooah and the executive who'd offered her a shot at a prime time series.

> **Though the etymology is in dispute, some scholars believe the word "abracadabra" comes from ancient Hebrew and means "I create as I speak." A good mantra for anyone starting up or starting over. You make things happen when you take action, which sometimes means finding the right plug for the right socket.**

Wadooah helped my client improve the treatment for the series. It's a document that includes the title, a two-line summary or logline, synopsis, episodes, and character descriptions. Treatments become pilots, then series, if all goes well. It's like a startup deck that leads to investment. You're just looking for someone to give you a green light.

After a few weeks, we were ready to pitch the series idea to Wadooah's contact, the chief prime time programming executive at one of the premier cable networks. I was prepared for everyone to say they loved it, even if they didn't. I'd been down this road before with the CHANT music entrepreneur.

The pitch meeting date was moved several times, and the anchor grew tired of changing her flights from New York to LA. She agreed to let us pitch it without her.

I had expected a few note takers and some more "suits" in the room, but it was only the executive, Wadooah, and me. We had 30 minutes to nail it. After 10 minutes, the executive's assistant came in with a note, an old trick meant to give the boss an escape in case the meeting was going south. The assistant was sent away, and our meeting stretched to 90 minutes.

We were clearly rank amateurs with no agency affiliation, but this executive wanted to help us: Wadooah and I were wide open to suggestions. We were given a "pitching" tutorial, including a homework assignment, a sign that we could expect another meeting. We were thrilled with the outcome, and no, I'm not going to reveal the executive's name or the network. It's possible the stars are lining up for our work with the network to resume after the anchor's new contract expires.

**Have you been given a once-in-a-lifetime opportunity to make a pitch? Are you ready? When meeting with someone who has a checkbook and knows more than you do about whether your idea is a fit, make sure you listen more than you talk. And take notes.**

Wadooah eventually launched an LGBTQ streaming service, then took a full-time job at Warner Media, where she stayed for three years. Today she has her own digital media consultancy, and we still refer business to each other.

If you nurture your network, you will connect deeply with some people. I've found, especially with women, business and friendship are fluid categories. Even if we haven't spoken in years, the women I've done business are all friends, and we'll still be there for each other in crises. We'll also find and refer opportunities to one another whenever we can.

The Southern California startup community stretches from Santa Barbara to San Diego, from the beach to the mountains. There's a vibrant startup scene in downtown LA (known as DTLA), Pasadena, and in other parts of LA county, but Santa Monica and Venice are preferred by a lot of founders, especially by those who surf. Cross Campus started there. It was one of the first shared workspace companies, and it hosts useful workshops and live events. Now they have 30 campuses in six countries.

General Assembly, which offers classes for people interested in learning tech skills, has provided good networking opportunities for my life among LA startups. WeAreLATech's Espree Devora, a podcast queen, has an office there. She and Kam Kashani are the connoisseurs of all things tech in LA. And they can plug you into the best entrepreneurs in town. If you're interested in cannabis businesses, Kristen Yoder of Soil to the Oil can help you whack your way through the forest of bad actors in that industry to find the OG startups.

Espree, Kam, and Kristen are three women who have nurtured their contacts through constant networking and introductions. Often, the people you meet at big events are "one and done." You have a great conversation, you exchange contact information, and nothing happens. But these women get it.

 **Follow up, if it's something that interests you. Don't expect people you meet to make the first move. Sometimes you'll meet people and get a deal done on the spot. Or in the first phone call. Other times, people need a little more time—or a deadline you set, after the initial consultation.**

Boundaries are essential when you're selling your brains, experience, and network. That's why consultants who have "productized" their services do so well. They offer a clear menu of choices for their potential clients, and those that don't commit are like an abandoned online shopping cart: Maybe they'll come back another day, but meanwhile you take care of your other shoppers. You want buyers, not spectators.

For any entrepreneur, it's critical to assess whether a potential client is worth pursuing or wasting your time. Put a form on your website that qualifies your leads by asking questions about budget, timeline, and the scope of work. Don't bother with people who try to get you to reduce your fees, unless they're overseas (in a market where your rates are not competitive). Or if it's a nonprofit or a campaign or a cause that matters to you, don't charge anything, if you can afford it. Better to volunteer than cheapen your brand.

# Chapter 23
# Referrals, Recommendations, and Why They're So Valuable

Soon after Margaret had finished middle school, I was surfing the Web, looking for alternative educational opportunities for her. I found a website called Workaway.info. This marketplace matches backpackers with work-exchange opportunities around the world.

I signed her up for an equestrian experiential learning program along the Garden Route outside of Cape Town, South Africa. She would spend her freshman year of high school living with a mother and daughter who owned horses. The daughter was a little older than Margaret, and she was training for the Olympics. I recalled how my summers living with families in Paraguay and Spain had helped expand my horizons and focus on my future. Even as I was eating pipas in the afternoons in Spain, I was learning valuable life lessons.

I wanted to send Margaret to a rural area to get her away from the bra-strap-and-belly-showing, weed-smoking, trash-talking, toxic culture of southern California high schools. Anglo teenage girls in LA are a band of skinny toddlers in tank tops. Maybe one day I'll write about that hellish period of my life: parenting a teenage girl in LA.

Margaret could have traveled to South Africa on her own. She'd spent part of the previous three summers at Copper Creek horse camp in the Sierra Mountains of northern California. But I confess I wanted the chance to connect with startup entrepreneurs in Cape Town, known as Silicon Cape. Margaret's life adventure would help expand her mom's startup network. I wanted to accompany her to establish my business footprint in Africa.

I reached out to a few founders, set up some meetings, and found a great airfare on Virgin, my favorite airline. I signed a startup software client in South Africa in advance of our trip, a company that offered a digital marketing platform for retailers. He'd hired me during our first phone call.

By the end of the summer, though, the Ebola epidemic was spreading outside of west Africa. South Africa had closed its borders to flights from the affected countries and Cape Town was far away from the outbreak, but the US media coverage terrified Margaret. We decided to postpone our trip. My work for the new client would have to continue online, and it worked out fine. It motivated me to join a Silicon Cape startup business group. I hope to get there eventually, and maybe Margaret will travel with me.

An engineer from Oslo reached out to me one day through LinkedIn. He told me he was an inventor who held patents for a half dozen consumer gadgets and tools and he wanted to talk to me about infomercials. The most interesting (and potentially marketable) item he told me about was a multipurpose Swiss

Army-style hammer, and he needed a prototype.

I immediately thought of a UK entrepreneur I'd recently met in LA. A personal trainer who owned a high-end gym in London, he had shown me a prototype of a trigger-point massage device meant to be used after workouts. He had designed and printed the prototype himself, on a 3D printer. I thought the graceful oval design, with the little knob at the end, was novel. He told me he was inspired by a toy he'd found in a sex shop in the Netherlands. I know, weird.

The multipurpose hammer inventor told me he didn't know of any 3D printers in Norway. I connected him to the gym owner in the UK and never heard from either of them again. In my fantasy, the two of them got together and created a multipurpose "Swiss Army" massager.

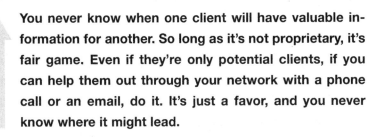

**You never know when one client will have valuable information for another. So long as it's not proprietary, it's fair game. Even if they're only potential clients, if you can help them out through your network with a phone call or an email, do it. It's just a favor, and you never know where it might lead.**

# Chapter 24
# Hey Bullies, Meet the White House Singer

I don't remember much I learned in high school except this: I finally realized that I deserved respect; I didn't have to earn it, I could just be myself.

The 1969 Supreme Court decision requiring public schools to desegregate was a blow to local parents who wanted their children to attend "all white" schools. They enrolled their children in private schools outside of the county, and the rest of us attended a new, integrated public high school six miles from my home.

For me, it was like moving to foreign country. New peers, new friendships, and a chance to ditch my reputation as the most unpopular student in school.

Dreaming of an exciting future as a recording artist, I joined the school chorus. When the choir director chose me as a soloist, I felt seen for the first time in my life by someone outside my family. Mr. Meier recognized my dedication to singing, and he decided to give me my shot. He encouraged me to trust my talent, and to disregard my inner critic.

Then he asked me to sing "Alfie" for a school assembly.

I wore a red velvet full-length dress with cap sleeves and a gathered bodice, gold sandals, and gold hoop earrings. My hair was long, freshly curled, and beautiful. I leaned against a wooden bar stool with a single key light shining down on me. I couldn't see the audience, but I could sense their presence in the dark.

The reel-to-reel tape player turned on and I hit all the notes. After sitting in complete silence during the whole song (a rarity for one of our assemblies), the applause from the audience filled my soul.

It was my moment, and I took a bow.

Thirty years later, I was in the middle of a busy day on a TV set when I answered a call on my cell phone from a South Carolina area code. It was an old classmate of mine, a girl who had not bullied me in elementary school, but had not defended me, either.

"Jeannie," she said, "I'm calling you because I want to apologize to you. All those years in elementary school when you were bullied, I never stood up for you and I'm ashamed. I am calling to tell you I am so sorry."

I nearly dropped the phone. She had found my number through a mutual friend and told me she had wanted to reach out to me for years. I was shocked, grateful, and happy to forgive her, though I had never blamed her for anything. The redemption felt good for both of us, and today I consider her a friend.

I've told the story many times since then and every time I do, it heals me a little more. My mother's advice when I was bullied, to "let it roll off your back like water off a duck's back," was some of the worst advice I've ever received. It's nearly impossible to do that as a child.

I forgave my friend, and I forgave the bullies. I know how lucky I am, and I've put it all behind me. Thank you, Faye, for your phone call. And thank you, Mr. Meier, for giving me a chance to shine as a singer. Without you, I never would have auditioned for Southern Singers in college, where I also became a soloist. And I never would have dared to sing professionally, if you hadn't given me my first opportunity.

 **Living well is not the best revenge: Feeling successful and confident after feeling neither, is.**

Fifteen years after my solo in the auditorium at Central High School I was invited to sing at a private party with my new band. The party was in the East Room of the White House. Here's how it happened.

It was 1977. My first week on the job at the InterAmerican Development Bank, I met George, a guitarist from Chile who was having lunch in the cafeteria. He told me he planned to travel home for the Viña del Mar international music festival the following year. He also told me he was looking for a singer for his Latin American band. I auditioned for him, and after I sang "Girl from Ipanema" in Portuguese, he said, "Congratulations. Welcome to Los Clasicos. We have a rehearsal tomorrow and a paid job on Saturday."

We played our first gig at an Italian restaurant in suburban Northern Virginia. George wailed on his favorite Les Paul guitar. A friend of George's, also from Chile, played bass, and we hired a much older Peruvian pianist to play piano. We couldn't afford a drummer, so we plugged in an electric drum machine. I sang and played the tambourine. There were a dozen people in the restaurant, and we made $35 each.

By the end of the year, we had performed at weddings, bar mitzvahs, and lavish embassy parties. We took a 10-piece band with horns, congas, and real drums to the Junior Diplomats Ball, the black tie New Year's Eve party for embassy staffers from around the world who were assigned to DC.

The ballroom of the historic Organization of American States building, three blocks from the White House was immense and beautifully decorated, with a huge stage and an echoey, distorted sound system. That didn't matter to the guests. After midnight the organizers kept asking us to play more sets. We were fine with that because it meant more of overtime pay. Each of us made $500 that night.

I was so pumped after the party, I decided to do something daring, even for me. I called the White House switchboard, and asked to speak to the social secretary. They put me through to Gretchen Poston. I knew this would be my one chance, and I didn't want to blow it.

I said this quickly, because I was afraid she would hang up on me.

"I have a band and we'd like to play in the White House. We just played the Junior Diplomats' party and they loved us."

And then she said, "Okay, the Carters have some friends traveling in Mexico. They're hosting a dinner for them when they get back next Sunday night. Can you come then?"

I thought I might have misheard her, but she was saying "Yes."

So, I said, "Yes."

When I told my band members they said: "Hey, man, how much are we getting paid?" I said "Nada. It's an honor to play in the White House."

They also worried about the Secret Service checking their immigration status, but I told them if they had a problem, they'd need to find a backup musician. No way I was going to risk losing this opportunity.

It was snowing heavily as I lifted the skirt of the elegant, peach-colored evening gown that I'd borrowed from my mother and walked through the diplomatic entrance to the White House, my band members trailing behind with their instruments. The social secretary had booked only a small combo, so we were back to our original four members of Los Clasicos. No drum machine this time.

I had grown up near the Mason-Dixon line, but had never been inside the White House. To arrive there as a performer and play for the Carters and their friends was a thrill. I kept thinking about how far I'd come since my high school performance of "Alfie." Then, it got even better.

As the Carters and their guests were heading downstairs to the screening room for a movie and we were packing up our instruments, Chip Carter tapped me on the shoulder.

"Mom would like to invite you all to have dinner here."

So, there I was, a guest in the East Room, the setting for most of the exclusive, elaborate dinners where the President and First Lady host foreign heads of state.

We were served on the Roosevelt china, and used the Lincoln silverware. How tempting was it to slip a fork in my purse? Extremely. One of the stewards gave us a tour of the kitchen; the State Dining Room, where they hold after dinner performances and press conferences; and a few other rooms not on the standard White House tour.

I have dined out on this story ever since.

Singing has always been my salvation, even if I don't have perfect pitch. When I was so sad and lonely in elementary school, my mom would play the piano for me so I could perform songs from Broadway musicals, holding a banana as a microphone. I told her I wanted to sing professionally when I grew up, but she told me, "Singers are a dime a dozen." I was crushed, but I never let go of that dream. I've managed to find plenty of opportunities to keep singing, though the older I get, the lower my voice gets. My soprano voice is now in the alto range, and sometimes I can even sing tenor.

In 2018, I joined the Selah Gospel Choir in Pasadena, California. We sang electrifying, heart-opening, gospel music. Those rehearsals and our Christmas performance were the high points of that year for me. This nonprofit choir draws people from all over Los Angeles county—all ages, all races, all genders, all religions and no religion. There's no audition required, so I don't know how the choir director got us to sound so good, but we did. If you live in the area and love to sing, sign up.

 **Do something you've always wanted to do or try something creative that you've never tried before. What are you waiting for? As the gospel song says: "Joy, Joy, Joy."**

I'm spending most of my time in Texas these days, and I've recently found a place to sing gospel music only 30 minutes from my house. Smoking for Jesus Ministry in Marble Falls. I'm SBNR (spiritual but not religious), but I am drawn to the energy and spirit of this church, founded by Katrina refugees. After they lost everything in the hurricane that hit New Orleans in 2005, a group of 200 church members caravanned out of there, ending up in the heart of the Hill Country, an unlikely sanctuary for Black families starting over with nothing. Members of the church assimilated into the mostly Caucasian community by sharing their culinary roots, through the highly regarded The Real New Orleans Restaurant.

> **Starting over is never easy, but sometimes it's your only choice. Imagine the courage it takes to uproot your family in search or a better life. Or to escape violence, unrest, or a natural disaster at home. Now imagine it with children in tow, hungry, exhausted, traveling on foot toward an uncertain future. Your fresh start will probably seem easy by comparison.**

I bow to the many startup founders I've worked with who are immigrants, and to the many, many others who long to return home but have been forced to start over in a new land.

# Chapter 25
# My Dad,
# The Wannapreneur

My father was an educated, compassionate idealist. An optimist with a perpetually sunny disposition. He wasn't the least bit shy around new people and was eager to make connections—not to expand his network for business reasons, but because he was genuinely interested in other people. His favorite response to "How are you?" was "Terrific. Really great. Can't complain at all."

His genuine smile and crackling laughter helped him put people at ease and built bridges with those who may not have agreed with him on anything besides the weather. Though trained in an adversarial profession—the law—he was pretty good at helping others find common ground with each other, and with him.

Dad was an active member of the Lions Club and he made a little extra income as the town attorney. He was a dear man who helped a lot of people, one of the few lawyers in the area in the 1950s who would represent Black clients, either pro bono or for a small fee.

This was still the old, segregated South: the balcony in the movie theater was reserved for "coloreds only," and the doctor's office had a "colored" waiting room with tattered red vinyl furniture and a "colored" drinking fountain. I remember questioning my mom about it and her reply, was "I know, it's wrong, but that's the way it is here." Like most kids my age, we accepted it as a fact of life, until our county finally had to fall in line with rest of the country and start recognizing civil rights by desegregating our schools.

Though we struggled financially, we were "town kids." We weren't required to do physical labor, as many of our classmates did on their family farms. Dad was one of the few licensed professionals in the county, and we all recognized that we had certain advantages. We were taught to appreciate what we had without complaining. We never missed a meal or had to forgo the purchase of a uniform or a musical instrument or make an excuse for not going on a class trip.

Dad would often read books in tandem: On his nightstand he'd have a biography alongside an autobiography of the same person, and history books that covered the same eras in different parts of the world.

He was a superhuman search engine. Whenever anyone in the family had a question, we'd ask him, and watch his brain boot up like an old computer. He could usually retrieve a useful fact, point us to further reading, and offer an astute observation. He probably would have been much happier as a journalist, and he would have been a great one. He didn't really enjoy practicing law, or the business of running a law practice. But he loved politics, and public service.

Dad and mom did their best to make their marriage work, and they loved each other, but they struggled for years to pay the bills. It took an emotional toll on both of them.

Mom had been the de facto CFO for the law office. She wanted him to refuse to do any additional work for clients whose bills were overdue. But my father didn't have the heart for it. I can remember desperately poor men in tattered wool jackets coming into his office in the middle of summer, holding their hats in their hands. These polite southern gentlemen had nowhere else to turn. They pleaded with him to help them get their social security payments straightened out, or to help them fill out some other government form. Find them some work. Help them with a domestic abuse case. Some of Dad's clients couldn't read or write, so they signed their papers with an X. As a country lawyer he was involved in all facets of the human condition: domestic abuse, tax problems, DUIs, even murder. When his clients paid, sometimes it was with their only currency: vegetables, ducks and chickens, family heirlooms.

Whenever a client brought in a check or cash, mom tried to make sure it went into the bank and didn't get spent on one of my dad's harebrained entrepreneurial ideas. He was a wannabe entrepreneur. Out of necessity, he was always trying to generate extra income by starting a new venture. Like boomerangs, which he made from plywood using an electric saw he'd bought and installed in our basement. Or partial ownership of a local gas station. Or a laundromat, or a restaurant, both of which were terrible investments for someone who was unfamiliar with those businesses. Or a winery. He'd built a grape arbor in the back yard, when he thought he might become a vintner, but he made one batch of muscatel wine that the neighbors deemed "undrinkable." Finally, after many attempts at entrepreneurship (today you might call him a "wannapreneur") and after three of us had gone to college, with the youngest in tenth grade, my parents divorced.

My darling dad was great at starting things up, even if they didn't go anywhere. He had the heart of an entrepreneur, and the mind of an academic. He wasn't afraid of hard work, he just wanted to be successful, and he didn't know how. He made some terrible mistakes, but he was my hero, and always, without fail, my advocate and my champion.

**Quick, extra income is not the best reason to become an entrepreneur. Working in the gig economy puts money in the bank faster and it's less risky, but you're limited by the number of hours you can devote to it. If you think you have a product or service that solves a problem, especially a problem you've experienced yourself, buckle up and prepare for a long ride with no additional income for a while.**

# Chapter 26
## First Jobs, Fainting

Though I was too young to be hired legally, Dad asked his friend Frank to give me my first "off the books" job the summer before my 14th birthday. I would run the tiny one-room pro shop at the local private golf, tennis and swim club, where somehow we had a family membership. (I don't know how my father pulled that one off—he must have done free legal work for the club.)

There was no register, so I safeguarded the cash in the cigar box. There was no adding machine, either. Whenever I made a sale, I had to do the math and calculate the tax on a piece of paper, so I could give customers the correct change.

On stormy summer afternoons when lightning kept golfers away from the course, after I'd swept and straightened the shelves, I'd sit around and cut open old golf balls with a pocket-knife, slicing through the rubber bands to the black foam core, piercing it with the edge to get to the salt water and corn syrup mixture inside. Even in a routine job, I found ways to keep myself busy and entertained.

I supplemented my $5 a day salary with a self-serve perk: a NuGrape soda and a pack of Planter's peanuts from the vending machine. Frank didn't mind. He and his buddies would retire to the main clubhouse after their rounds, for some 19th hole action. This was a dry county, so club members had lockers where they stored their whiskey, which they would mix with sodas they bought from the pro shop. Nothing like a spiked Mountain Dew to take your mind off of that putt you missed.

It was a sweet life that summer. I rode my bike two miles each way in the brutal heat and humidity, knowing how lucky I was to be out of school, earning my own money.

It was not an important job, but as my dad used to say, "Never be ashamed of any job you do. All work is honorable." The pro shop job gave me a head start in the world of work. My boss taught me how to greet customers and treat them well, so they'd feel special.

My next seasonal job, in retail, offered bonuses and additional incentives, and it taught me how to sell. In my junior and senior years of high school, I worked in the town's nicest clothing store: Oakley & Lee. The salary was low, but a 10 percent commission on every sale awakened a strong desire to compete with the other salesclerks. I coveted the hefty commissions I saw the guys rack up on men's suits, hats, and shoes. I knew I'd have to scramble to get my sales totals up from the ladies shopping for church hats, new shoes, and gifts for their kids.

It was a small town, and everybody knew who had money to spend. Whenever someone walked in, I would calculate their potential commission value, and either attach myself to them, or let them go. But there were adults working there who depended on their paychecks to feed their families. I'm sure they were relieved when summer was over, and the student workers like me went back to school.

One day, shortly after I had been vaccinated for my trip to Paraguay, I was showing a customer a pair of white calfskin gloves with pearl buttons. I remember she was having a hard time getting them off and I came around to the front of the display case to help her. The next thing I knew I felt the cold linoleum floor on my back and something wet behind my head. I had fainted, hit my head on the glass front of the display case, and lay there in a pool of blood. I could hear the customer calling out to my boss, saying, "Hey, the girl fell." After contacting my mother, Mr. Lee lifted me up and walked to me out of the front door where my mom picked me up and drove me two blocks to doctor's office.

Dr. Baugh cut off a big chunk of my hair and gave me two shots in the back of my head. As he stitched me up he kept telling me how brave I was. It was the same speech he had given me when I was a toddler, when he'd put six stitches around my eye. I had fallen on our wooden staircase at home and ripped the delicate skin on a protruding nail. The scar on my eye has faded, but my hair has a weird part in the back from the display case injury.

 **Medical drama almost always occurs when you least expect it. Learn the Heimlich, take a CPR course, be a first responder in your workplace. Maybe you'll like it enough to change careers.**

# Chapter 27
## Falling into Writing

TV guest bookers need networking skills, persistence, and sharp elbows. Journalist Jane Mayer wrote about some of my most exciting and competitive experiences as a booker when she was a cub reporter at *The Wall Street Journal*. I was also interviewed on *Entertainment Tonight* and appeared in a segment on ABC's *20/20*.

My friend and former NBC colleague Shelley Ross told her pal Rudy Maxa about some of my most extreme experiences as a guest booker, including the time I got held up by machine gun in El Salvador. At the time Rudy wrote for *The Washington Post*, which ran full-page interviews with newsmakers and other notable Washingtonians, in the Sunday Outlook section. He thought my stories were interesting enough to pitch doing a profile on me, and his editor gave him the green light.

I was over 30, desperate to get married, not dating anyone. I was excited to do the interview, thinking it would be catnip for DC's eligible single men.

Wrong! The only person who reached out to me was Lois Lindstrom, the press secretary for the Senate Republican Campaign Committee. She asked if I would come up to the Hill to speak to Republican press secretaries about how to get their bosses on TV. I agreed, again, hoping I might get a date out of it. But no, no luck.

A few months after my interview appeared, I approached Rudy's editor about freelancing for the *Post*. He gave me two assignments, also profiles for the Sunday Outlook section: one with the wickedly funny public affairs officer for the CIA, Herb Hetu, and the other with Michael Robinson, director of the National Zoo. Herb was entertaining but revealed no secrets. Michael posed for his profile photo with his pet kinkajou.

 **Be audacious. You might get turned down, but why not try? If you pick a good target and make a strong case, you might get a good response.**

The Post profiles were Q&As with a lead-in of only a few paragraphs, but having a byline in a respected newspaper opened the door to more freelance writing. I would write for a few other publications after that. So long as I have a brain and a keyboard, freelance writing is an additional revenue stream for my business.

Since my handwriting was nearly illegible, I avoided writing in my formative years in school. The typewriter changed everything. I'm grateful to Mr. Brown, who taught me typing in the eighth grade. Our new school had the latest IBM Selectrics and a new product called Liquid Paper. It was hot and noisy in our classroom, but I could hear echoes of my mother's strong "suggestion" that typing would take me places.

Writing requires a tremendous amount of ass sitting. Procrastinating is part of the craft. I certainly excel at that. But there's nothing better than reading pages that have been tweaked and massaged and sweated over for years. Yes, I'm talking about this book, which I started writing in 2014. It's taken me a while, I know.

I'm doing my best here.

The most important piece of advice in this book that I hope you will follow is this: What is your career? Engineer? Artist? Entrepreneur? No matter what you say you are, you have to communicate with others.

 **Learn to write. Practice daily. Read widely, across cultures and genres. Writing well is a ticket to upward mobility. A well-crafted letter can land you a job, get you a promotion, or change a judge's mind. It can also heal a broken heart, lift someone's spirits, and set things right.**

Elizabeth Gilbert said recently in a podcast interview that Julia Cameron's *The Artist's Way* lit the fuse for her to write *Eat, Pray, Love*. Cameron's book lays out a 12-week plan for unblocking your creativity, and I can testify that it is life changing. And it's not only meant for artists and writers.

We're all creatives. Professions that may not seem so can be more creative than they appear. Startup founders. Scientists. Farmers. Bankers. Lawyers. Auto mechanics. Waitresses. Accountants. Engineers. Sex workers. Think about it. The best ones are problem-solvers. And how do you solve a problem? With creative thinking? It's more than that. It's about recognizing that you're a channel for the river of creativity that is constantly flowing. Ideas are brought forth through you, not from you. And if you're stuck, whether it's writer's block or solving a problem, stop thinking in the traditional sense and take a step back. The result? Creative solutions will flow. That's why some of our best ideas come to us just before we go to sleep, or in the car, or in the shower.

During the times I've been "inside," as opposed to freelancing or involved in an entrepreneurial venture, I've reviewed plenty of résumés and cover letters with stupid sentences, typos, and other idiocy. If someone had a typo in a cover letter, I rejected them. I've made mistakes like that myself, but I am a hard-ass when I hire someone. If I find a typo in this book after it goes to print, it will make me crazy.

**If you have a learning disability like dyslexia or ADD, you may have difficulty spelling. It's okay. Triple check your work, and read each page backwards, word by word. It's a great way to catch typos and spelling errors. And be sure to take advantage of Spellcheck.**

Mobile messaging makes allowances for all sorts of spelling and abbreviation anomalies. It's easy for us older adults to bemoan the lack of younger generations' difficulty spelling and reading maps. New communication platforms drive changes in the language, and if my peers don't keep up, we'll look like old fools. This explains why I sometimes use emojis and the occasional LOL.

# Chapter 28
## Dumb Mistakes, and Good Decisions

For my starter marriage, I chose a husband as if I were hiring an employee. Strong résumé, bright future, presentable to "clients"— my friends and family. Marrying a Harvard/Stanford/MIT/ Fletcher guy was an achievement for a small-town girl. His baggage was less important to me than his brain and his brawn.

Husband No. 1, Doug, was extremely intelligent, well-traveled and well-read, funny, sensitive, and a deep thinker. He said he loved me, but he was too broken by a series of losses in his young life to be in a committed relationship. He was only affectionate in the first year or two of our nine-year marriage. We were together constantly, traveled often, and had lots of adventures, but I was lonely. My first marriage was a mistake, yet I don't regret the years I spent with Doug. Neither of us expected it to end that way.

Ironically, I met Husband No. 2, Don, and Husband No. 1 in the same month in 1985. But the wisdom of the gods blessed us with more time for personal growth before No. 2 and I would discover, in 1997, that we were destined to be together.

We'd each married other people in 1987. We'd both traveled around the world and were divorcing our respective spouses 10 years later. Don had leased a condo on the beach in Malibu while writing a screenplay with his son about a Black basketball player who runs for President and wears sponsor patches on his suits like a NASCAR driver. Maybe we should ask all our elected officials to do that today.

I was living in a guesthouse on the other end of Malibu, partying it up with my single friends. I've already told you the story of how Don and I reconnected and soon after got pregnant, then moved to San Francisco, and married. The first few years of late-in-life parenting had been pure bliss in our apartment overlooking the Golden Gate bridge.

When Margaret was five years old, after we'd tried the East Coast again and returned to sunny weather in Malibu, we moved to beautiful, bucolic and weirdly wonderful Topanga, the spiritual capital of Southern California. It's a magical enclave that is hard to appreciate unless you live there. We leased a 30-acre ranch with a small, comfortable house that had floor-to-ceiling windows: Rabbits, deer, and the occasional coyote paraded in front of the living room window. It was like watching a nature show every evening at dusk.

I homeschooled Margaret from first grade until she entered school at age 10. It was a good decision. As homeschooling parents know, it's an enormous time and emotional commitment. It's also an educational journey you take together with your child. It can be very rewarding, so long as you're not trying to juggle a job at the same time, as many parents had to do in 2020 and 2021.

More than 30 other families were homeschooling in

Topanga in 2003, so we didn't feel Margaret would suffer from social isolation. She and I spent one day a week at home, doing assignments handed out by a teacher from the Las Virgenes school district. The rest of the week we were free to join the other families on field trips or "park days." We also found wonderful enrichment classes, including civics, Shakespeare, dance, chess, and a combined French language, theatre arts, and magic class taught by Mademoiselle Coco.

When I wrote the first draft of this book, Margaret was 16. She'd completed middle school, and it would be at least seven more years until her brain's frontal lobes would fully mature. Almost every day had brought a renewed battle over money, clothes, weed, schoolwork, foul language, noise, cleaning her room, and whatever other drama was unfolding. With both parents working from home and, a teenager on independent study, we were tripping over each other, relying on a family therapist to help level us so that Margaret could find her way to graduation or at least a GED.

After years of flying around the world and staying in five-star hotels, here Don and I were, in a small apartment trying to survive the next few years together. The drama of the teen years had involved law enforcement, rehab, crystals, natural remedies, medication, meditation, and lots of family therapy.

 **Stuff happens. Try to remain calm. At times it's easier to have full-time employment, but entrepreneurship or a consulting practice can give you the flexibility to deal with the occasional emergency, and sometimes intractable family problems.**

My failures as a wife and as a mother would take more than a chapter to enumerate, but here are a few.

I spent too much time with my laptop open, half-listening and not enough time cooking. When we all ate together, I inhaled the relief, the calm in the household. Mom's in the kitchen, and in this family, at least, that felt like normal life. Moods were much improved, conversations were had about safe topics, and deposits in the bank of good feelings grew. It was our restorative spiritual practice. Don did laundry, vacuumed, and other chores. It was an arrangement that worked for us and provided some stability amid the chaos.

I was always too lenient as a parent, in part because Don, whose childhood was unhappy, resorted to a 1950s authoritarian style of parenting. This was usually accompanied by a fair amount of volume. I believed a child needed at least one good cop parent, and I often lacked the fortitude or the energy to say "no."

This ended up creating a perfect storm for the "divide and conquer" strategy of a wily only child. Having her carom back and forth against our different parenting styles created nothing but confusion and stress for all of us. If you're parenting like this, take notice.

"The problem is you've never shown her who's the boss," said my mother, who left no doubt as to who wore the pants in my family when I was growing up. But she never had a kid like this, and only parents of kids like this will understand. Extremely bright kids with some learning differences such as ADD manifest as "low output" and are therefore labeled "lazy." Plus there was anxiety, depression, and PTSD that we could never trace to its source. Early and frequent use of cannabis probably made things worse for her. I'm an advocate for legal cannabis, but the research shows it can be harmful to teenage brains.

Personal regrets as a parent are many, and I don't think there's a parent alive who doesn't have some. I feel your pain.

**Failure is a gift wrapped in barbed wire. It wounds us. We bleed, but it's not fatal. Startups fail, relationships fail, parenting fails, yet we persist because we have to. The gift of failure is information. It informs our decision-making going forward, and it gives us a chance to make new choices, which will, in time, lead to better outcomes.**

Someone should create a parody of LinkedIn called "Behind My Profile." It would have the same profile pictures, with opportunities to connect and provide endorsements, but instead of a chronological listing of career highs it would list career lows, mistakes, and firings.

I've already opened the kimono for you now. Why not go ahead and toss it on the bonfire?

Here are some truths Behind My Profile:

▼ Graduated ninth in my high school class, with a B+ average. I could have done better. School just wasn't my thing.

▼ B student in college. See above.

▼ Engaged in wildly inappropriate conversations with superiors at NBC (in the bad old days, before #metoo).

▼ Had a brief fling with a married journalist (we were in a war zone, but still, no excuse).

▼ Impersonated a hostage family member. Got into a memorial service at Andrews Air Force Base. Secured an interview for Dan Rather (totally unethical, so a personal failure, but it was my hero moment at the *CBS Evening News*). Well, maybe I don't regret this.

▼ Misplaced my script notes for an important and super-secret shoot. I was convinced they were stolen from my car, so I filed a police report. I discovered I had left them in my friend's café the night before. I had to inform the production company, which had to tell the client, who then put the multi-million-dollar account up for review due to the "security breach."

Okay. That's enough.

Making the wrong decisions is a rite of passage in the startup community. Startup founders understand the concept of falling down seven times, getting up eight. Regrettable choices are not a sign of stupidity. We're human. How well you learn from them is the measure of your character. It's a blueprint for your future success, as well as a lesson in humility.

Whether it's the economy, the shortage of available jobs, or a sense of ennui after years in corporate careers, people over 45 are starting most of the new businesses these days. As more boomers retire, I expect the age of new entrepreneurs will rise, too.

As an advisor and consultant to small startup companies, I have finally found my groove. A lifetime of scanning the horizon as a journalist and as a curious, would-be renaissance woman, has given me the tools I need to be a Startup Jeannie. I can carefully and quickly assess a business, its challenges and growth opportunities.

I've traded stability for invention and reinvention of my professional self, but my soul self has remained constant. I'm a small-town girl who brought her A-game to the big city, satisfied her wanderlust, and ended up with a foot in both worlds. I split my time between homes in the Texas Hill Country and Southern California, and I work with startups wherever they call home.

My shortcomings, failures, and disappointments have given me freedom to take the risks I've had to take to be successful. So, what if I fail again? I'll keep trying.

# Chapter 29
# My Daughter,
# The Startup Artist

When Margaret was born, I expected to look into her eyes and feel an instant connection, a recognition that this was truly my child. Instead, she was a stranger, a little Buddha. A wise old soul ready to take on the world. I loved her, of course, but I was more than a little intimidated. Maybe it was my erratic post-partum hormones, but I imagined her saying, "OK, I'm here now. Everybody out of my way: I'm on a mission." Born in the year of the tiger, she has her father's fiery spirit and my mother's chutzpah, my dad's amiability and sophisticated sense of humor, and a heart so big you'd think she had two of them.

She worried me sick when she was a teenager. Sometimes I wondered if she'd live to see her 18ᵗʰ birthday. I feared that one day I'd find her living on the street, or worse, I wouldn't find her at all. She never ran away from home, which surprised me: She was so rebellious, she was not about to be controlled by anyone, including, and perhaps especially, her parents. We had no idea she was stigmatized in school just because of her voluptuous body type, and worse, that she was suffering from physical and emotional abuse in her relationships. Abuse survivors are good at covering up their wounds and pretending their lives are okay, even as they desperately try anything to numb their pain.

One afternoon in 2016, when Don was in the ICU in LA recovering from brain surgery, I sat with her in an emergency room 20 miles away. It was our second time there in a month. Things couldn't get any worse, I thought.

Then, six months later, Margaret ended up in the ER again. That day, fortunately, she got the "God shot." It's not something administered by doctors; it's the sudden realization that this was not the life she wanted for herself. Finally, the "God shot" helped her reclaim her power.

A few months into her recovery, a friend taught her how to do tricks with hula hoops (now recognized as one of the "flow arts") and how to dance with fire props without getting burned. Losing herself in the swirling circles, and in the flames, brought her a sense of calm and balance: She was smitten. It's not that she wanted to run away and join the circus, she had found a reverence for being "in the flow," and she treasured the new friends she made in the communities of flow artists that welcomed her wherever she traveled.

Margaret enrolled in college but sitting in class and studying felt like barriers to the life she imagined as an artistic free spirit, a 21st century hippie. I bought her a backpack and a ticket to Costa Rica, feeling in my bones that she would rise to the challenge of traveling solo, even in a country where she didn't speak the language. I had found a Workaway opportunity for her at a hostel in Manzanillo, then as a receptionist and kitchen helper at a yoga retreat. Both would give her a sense of purpose, a safe community, and free room and board.

Within a month, she got herself hired as a fire performer in local clubs in Puerto Viejo, then traveled all over the country spinning her fire fans and double staffs for tips. She volunteered at the Envision Festival (jumping onstage to perform the last day) and connected with the members of Pyrodanza, one of the top fire dance troupes in the world. These professionals took her under their wing, taught her a few tricks and gave her some welcome companionship. They even welcomed her to their creative space near Tamarindo. Then she continued her travels through Panama, Colombia, and Mexico for the next nine months.

Along this journey, she taught herself to upcycle clothes for other performers using only a pair of scissors, which could double as protection while she traveled by herself. She also started an Instagram business, @ThirdEyeRiptie. Shameless plug from her mother. Product placement is everything.

After returning to the US in August, 2019, she volunteered at the Omega Institute for Holistic Studies in New York. One of the other volunteers introduced her to the legendary trans-cendental artists, Alex and Allyson Grey. She was thrilled to have the opportunity to fire dance at COSM, their Chapel of Sacred Mirrors, a mecca for seekers and artists from around the world.

No matter what art form feeds their soul, people in the creative arts have to eat and pay rent, too, and I've found they're natural entrepreneurs. The successful ones figure out how to commercialize their art without compromising their artistic vision. It's a constant battle for creatives, who feel compelled to bring ideas to life without any expectation of how their work will be received. I can see now that Margaret has the range and the appetite for risk, the talent, the vision, and the determination to fulfill her purpose on the planet, and she can use her interpersonal skills to keep getting herself hired and build her clothing line. One day soon, she may pick a lane, or not, but right now she's doing what she was meant to do in her early 20s: experiment and explore.

My little artist/entrepreneur has started up a range of creative endeavors, from recording music with the young man she met and fell in love with at Omega, to writing and producing her own songs. As @pyrodiosa (Fire Goddess) and @margiflows, she has an impressive list of performing credits, she's been invited to perform in Mexico for Diplo, in Austin and around the hill country, and may soon start teaching hooping and freestyle dance at a local studio.

As of this writing, her clothing business is growing so fast she's afraid she can't keep up with all the requests for custom orders. She's overwhelmed by the creative smorgasbord in front of her. Should she pursue a career as a fashion designer? Singer? Lyricist? Flow artist? Horse trainer? Writer? She's not sure, but she's still young. The business side of entrepreneurship may be daunting, but it's the missing link between where she is now and scaling her business. She's bootstrapped it all, putting together a diverse team of brand ambassadors, and has bartered her clothing for some business services. After a half dozen collaborations with other small clothing companies, a fashion designer contacted her this month to collaborate on a new line of luxury, one-of-a-kind costumes for performers. She is on her way in the fashion industry, if that's what she ultimately decides to do.

As Margaret grows it will be helpful to have someone else handle her supply chain and fulfillment, plus a full time social media manager/digital marketer. The worst part about having an e-commerce business is that she's always on her phone, which she recognizes is not good for her mental health. Meanwhile she is de facto CEO, designer, and customer service representative. She wears her ThirdEyeRiptie clothing in her hoop and fire performances, considering them sacred healing ceremonies as well as marketing opportunities. How many startup founders can say their companies are also their therapy? A fortunate few.

Like a phoenix, Margaret has risen from the ashes of her past, and it has imbued her with a deep empathy for others, along with a preternatural attraction to fire. Funny that her dad's glassblowing at Penland and her journey through the flow arts brought them both close to the flames. It's not surprising, though. We used to own horses, and the minute she "caught air" jumping over fences, she was hooked. She's adventurous and says taking risks makes her feel more alive. So long as she can find someone to ground her with business skills, she will make it as an entrepreneur.

 **Short-term, part-time help can put you on a path to faster growth. Competitors with deeper pockets can surpass you even if your product or service is better. If you're first to market, don't squander your head start. If you're entering a competitive market, learn from your competitors' mistakes and keep an eye on what they're doing, but don't obsess.**

# Chapter 30
## Chasing the Shiny Objects

When was the last time you gave yourself the gift of a challenge? Confronted your doubts about your intellectual, entrepreneurial, or creative abilities? Did you sign up for an art class? Join a choir? Hire a life coach?

Is it time for you to take on something new?

Ten years ago, I signed up for private fencing lessons in Malibu, taught by a professional coach named Igor.

I had no expectations and zero knowledge of the sport. Yet from the moment I suited up, pointed my sword at my opponent, and shouted "En garde!" I felt what I can only describe as "vertically aligned." It was an out-of-body experience. I could feel a sense of history and power, a timelessness and a desire to perfect the form so I could relive something I surely must have experienced in a past life.

I felt like Joan of Arc.

Fencing is a competitive sport, but it's also a kinetic art, and the fencer inhabits a complex world. Centuries of legendary duals. The science of movement. Techniques of deception. It requires extreme focus, speed, agility, strength, planning, and strategy. Left-handedness is an advantage, since most fencers are right-handed. I was a natural. I was captivated.

And how many classes did I take? Two.

Why didn't I stick with it? Life happens. No regrets.

But just taking those two lessons reminded me that when you're doing something you were born to do, it's almost effortless. It's flow. It's what Steven Kotler and others have successfully commercialized and packaged so that anyone can achieve this state in sports, music, business, writing—anywhere that demands peak performance.

After years starting and building companies, and other projects with very small teams, and now after a decade of being a "Startup Jeannie" I am living my daily life in what I would call a steady micro-dose of the flow state. It feels like a state of grace.

Part of that is genetic. I am blessed with the opposite of anxiety and depression: extreme serenity. And now, gratitude. It all informs how I work with clients, and the companies I mentor.

Following are just a few of the nearly 100 companies I have advised, mentored, worked for, or helped start. A more complete list appears in the back of the book. Many of them will have gone to that great startup incubator in the sky by the time you read this. Starting a company is a leap across the chasm from the known to the unknown: It's exciting, terrifying, exhausting, it consumes your life, and even if it doesn't succeed, in my experience it's worth a try.

The startup that will always be first in my heart is Ruby Rockets. The experience of helping to move a product made in someone's home kitchen to the shelves in retail stores was one of the most significant business challenges I've ever undertaken. I still own stock in the company, so of course I'm going to mention them first!

Another heartthrob is a French fashion designer in Beverly Hills, Igal Benhamou. Igal is manifesting his dream of creating a lifestyle brand with his beautiful line of hip, relaxing "meditation wear," a future meditation studio, and CBD tea, to get you in the mood. Always on trend, he's added mushroom tea to his product line. He hosts intimate, stylish events for the Instagram crowd, so watch for his announcements of upcoming mini-retreats at places like Jungl in LA. I helped Igal reposition his brand from the name "Believe or Leave" to simply "BOL," and prepared his business for due diligence from investors.

Jennifer Goldman is a New York entrepreneur who reminds me of Igal: She has such a big vision for her new company, Braveseed. It's a wellness platform centered on her proprietary line of mood-enhancing essential oils, inspirational speeches, and, in the future—courses and seminars, books, and community. I was on her mentor team for the startup accelerator BeyondSKU in New York. We helped Jennifer relaunch her brand, build her team, and prepare for an investment.

A team of mentors (who advise startup companies for 8–12 weeks at no charge) can make or break a fledgling startup, and Jennifer is one of the lucky few who made it into the BeyondSKU accelerator. She learned a lot in a short time from her mentor team members like the founder of Plum Organics, the former CEO of Dr. Hauschka skin care, a private equity guy, a lawyer, an e-commerce specialist, and me.

Noir D'Or, is a company I've been mentoring for Capital Factory. It's a skin repair system for people of color. I wasn't aware of this but having more melanin in your skin presents special challenges that other skin care companies have not effectively addressed. Jarrod and Ceci have been running the company out of their home in Houston for two years and have grown the business organically to nearly 100,000 customers. Now is the time for them to spread their wings and soar.

I've also mentored two cannabis companies for Capital Factory. These entrepreneurs have a base in Texas, but they work in Oklahoma. At this writing, Oklahoma is a great market for cannabis entrepreneurs. There are more than 3,000 dispensaries in the state, and the laws are much more friendly than the tax and regulatory mess that is California in 2021.

I'm very interested in the commercialization of plant medicines for the mental health market. I've introduced investors to EI Ventures, a startup company based in Maui that has spent 10 years building toward the launch of a brand in psychedelics— in particular psilocybin mushrooms. The founder of Psilly™, David Nikzad, is a serial entrepreneur and investor himself. At this writing he says he's taking 100 calls a week from investors all over the world who want to get into his industry. The ones that see pure dollar signs are not of interest to David. He's on a mission to help the millions of people with mental health problems who could benefit from righteously sourced, tested, and produced, psilocybin capsules, which he wants to offer for $1 a dose, once it is decriminalized. At this writing, Denver; Santa Cruz; Washington, DC; and the state of Oregon have all decriminalized psilocybin for therapeutic use.

These are powerful medicines, and though I haven't tried them (yet) I have seen the evidence from the trials at Johns Hopkins, and at Kings College in the UK: These plant medicines, properly administered and regulated, have the potential to help a lot of people with addiction and PTSD.

After advising and consulting for CreatorUp, the digital media company in LA, I mentored Abigail Baez of Blended Sense, another company that does digital content creation. While CreatorUp has had large contracts with Google, Special Olympics, and educational companies, Abbie is growing her business by creating rich video content for small businesses, starting in Austin.

Also in Austin are KOYA, a kindness app I am mentoring for Capital Factory, and mmmpanadas, an empanada company I mentored as part of a team for SKU Dallas. Both are run by entrepreneurs who want to build businesses that help people live better by spreading kindness and, in the latter case, offer healthy convenience food. For Expert Dojo I recently mentored companies in Cairo, New Delhi, Bucharest, Tallin, Johannesburg, and Vancouver.

Is your head spinning yet?

The world is full of things that need fixing, problems to be solved.

The world is waiting for you to get started. Or start over.

What are you waiting for?

# Postscript

The original title of this book was *Skipping Work*. When you love what you do, your work is a joy, not a chore. You're not actually skipping working; you're just skipping boredom. And that can make you feel like skipping. Remember when you learned to skip when you were a kid? And then when your mom told you not to run, you skipped? That's the feeling.

If you can find a way to skip "work" by working at something you love, you win. Skip whatever bad parts you can: the awful boss, the horrible commute, the monotony. Network like crazy. Follow your heart. Find your bliss. Don't look back. Get re-trained. Pursue that certificate or degree. You don't want to end up regretting the chances you didn't take. Even if you're healthy, who knows how long you have left to fulfill your life's purpose?

In April 2016, my husband, Don, the political consultant, got up in the middle of the night and fell. I had to help him get back in bed. The next morning, I noticed he was having trouble lifting his fork at breakfast. He didn't seem to recognize what the fork was used for. I took him to the emergency room. After a CT scan and MRI, the doctor looked back and forth at both of us. She spoke in an alarmingly calm tone of voice.

"It's good you came in today. Very good."

Doctors.

Don was diagnosed with stage 4 glioblastoma, the deadliest form of brain cancer. Five days later he had surgery to remove what his doctor called "an angry tumor." The surgery was considered successful. But after chemo, radiation, and more chemo, nothing was shrinking new tumor growth.

We signed up for home hospice at the end of September. He died October 11, at 69: he had always said he was surprised he'd lived past 60. When he realized the end was near, he was ready. An avid "river rat" who used to love to run rapids, I told him his bed was a raft that would take him home. I promised I would be beside him and hold his hand until the end. His death at home was beautiful and peaceful, and I'm so grateful to the warm-hearted, professional hospice team from Kaiser in LA.

Don was my soul mate and my hero. He was the most honest, hardworking, standup guy I had ever known, and that's an achievement for someone who spent most of his career in politics.

His death was not a shock; the diagnosis was. As anyone who's been through a terminal illness with a loved one will understand, my grieving started the moment we got the heartbreaking news in April. I had the privilege and blessing of a long goodbye.

Our daughter suffered terribly as she watched him dying at home. But she eventually found comfort in her father's philosophy of life that he'd shared with her over the years. Don was born Jewish, but always described himself as a Taoist/Buddhist/Animist. He'd helped us both understand that resisting change is always futile. Acceptance and love are everything. In spite of our sorrow, or perhaps because of our loss, my daughter and I have both grown as individuals, and we've grown closer to each other. When I first fell in love with Don, I told him he had "perfected the art of freelancing." He was so fearless about starting up, whether it was a new campaign, a new business, or writing a screenplay. He worked in his beach clothes at a glass-topped table overlooking the ocean, made a few phone calls, did a few projects, and only took clients when he felt like it. I was in awe.

Unfortunately, the dark side of that carefree lifestyle was a Peter Pan attitude about money. "It will come. It just gets better. You'll see." He'd say that whenever we were running low, sometimes the phone would ring, and he'd get another six-figure contract. Too often it didn't, and he'd borrow from family or friends to get us through the next month.

Living with him was a roller coaster, from lengthy stays at Fairmont hotels to broccoli & cheese–baked potatoes for dinner. But I don't have a single regret. He didn't, either. He lived his life on his own terms, starting up and starting over, again and again, for 45 years in business. He spoke often of how blessed he was.

Throughout this book I've told you about friends and colleagues who've chosen to start companies or start over—some high risk like ours, some who chose more conventional career paths. Though I enjoy working on teams and have almost always been happy in my office jobs, I could never picture myself spending decades in one company, or even in one industry. I'm too energized by new ideas, new people, and new experiences. My unconventional career path was my destiny. I'm glad it has given me such an exciting professional life at this stage of my career.

David Epstein's book *Range*, mentioned earlier, describes why people like me—expert generalists—can be so successful in the new world of work. We have so many different skills, knowledge, experience, and expertise—we have worn many hats—and that's particularly useful for startup companies. My work history qualifies me as someone with deep experience in starting up and starting over.

These days, I'm challenging myself to take the brakes off my self-limiting beliefs and go for large consulting contracts, like Don did. For years I'd thought he was the only one capable of doing that but now I think, why not me?

I learned so much from Don. The biggest gift he left me was a fierce courage, to add to my optimism and endless curiosity.

When her dad was in the hospital, Margaret posted a powerful quote from Angela Davis on her social media: "You'll never know how strong you are until being strong is your only choice." In the end, we have so little control over the events in our lives. Loss and grief eventually come to everyone, and we're all headed to the same place one day.

Be fearless. Stay strong.

And let me know how it goes.

startupjeannie@gmail.com

# But Wait: There's More!

The trouble with writing a memoir is you're not dead yet. More stuff happens. Some things just need to be mentioned before I end this book.

I'm still riding the rapids of reinvention. While continuing to work with startups in LA, Kamy Akhavan, then CEO of ProCon.org, hired me to raise money for his organization. This nonprofit bought half my time and stole much of my heart. It's a Web portal that helps people understand the rationale behind different points of view on controversial issues: immigration, gun control, abortion, and more. They were recently acquired by Encyclopedia Britannica, Inc.

Today I'm still doing consulting work for startup companies, and I'm an advisor for a documentary series, *Sanatione*. It's a collection of stories from the pandemic, shot, written and directed by local auteurs in 22 countries. It's starting as a Web series but may one day come to a theater near you. I connected the producers to Kathy Eldon at Creative Visions, an incubator for social impact films, based in Malibu. I can't help myself: I see a plug, and I have to find a socket. Always.

I still advise (paid) and mentor (gratis) startup founders in the US and overseas.

And the best of all?

On October 1, 2017, I started over again, with yet another

veteran entrepreneur. On that day, by the end of lunch at Marmalade Cafe, Dave Marshall and I both knew our lives were about to change for the better.

Did he invest in me? No.

Did I 10X his company? No.

We fell in love one week after connecting through a dating app. And every year our relationship seems to 10X itself.

There you go. Heart skipping. Starting over.

Happy ending.

END

# Startups to Watch

This is a partial list of companies I have mentored, advised, or consulted for over the last ten years. All of them are still in business as of this writing, but you know how it goes. By the time you read this, some of them may have pivoted, or gone away. Some may have even changed their names. As my agile percussionist friend, Taku Hirano says: T. A. K. U. Try and Keep Up!

## Beauty, Health and Wellness

**BOL:** https://believeorleave.com/
**BraveSeed:** (Coming in 2022)
**FitGuru:** https://www.fitguru.us/
**Kanthaka:** https://mykanthaka.com/
**Noir D'or Cosmetics:** https://noirdor.com/
**Petal:** https://withpetal.com/
**Shaz & Kiks:** https://www.shazandkiks.com/
**TINGE:** https://tingebeauty.com/
**Troupe Beauty:** https://troupebeauty.com/
**WeStrive:** https://www.westriveapp.com/

## Digital Media

**360 VR Technology:** https://360vrtechnology.com/
**Astronomic Agency:** https://www.astronomic.agency/
**Blended Sense:** https://www.blendedsense.com/
**CreatorUp:** https://creatorup.com/
**Fireshow Media:** https://www.fireshowmedia.com/

## Food and Beverage

Agua Bonita: https://www.drinkaguabonita.com/

Mmmpanadas: https://mmmpanadas.com/

Potli: https://www.getpotli.com/

Ruby Rockets: https://www.rubyrockets.com/

Xicama: https://xicamalife.com/

## Plant Medicines

El Ventures: https://www.ei.ventures/

Kanna (now OKO): https://www.oko.co/

Purple Unicorn: https://www.purpleunicorn.la/

Service Ganja: https://www.serviceganja.com/

## Tech

Ahlo: https://www.sayahlo.com/

Blue Roof Labs: https://www.bluerooflabs.com/

BodyDoubler: https://www.bodydoubler.com/

CommonAlly: https://www.commonally.com/

CustomerXI: https://customerxi.com/

Eisana Corp: https://eisana.com/

Explorastay: https://www.explorastay.com/

Fetii, Inc.: https://www.fetiiride.com/

Gardenio: https://www.growgardenio.com/

Gozova, Inc.: https://gozova.com/

KOYA Innovations: https://getkoya.com/

MealAlly: http://www.mealally.com/

MEAZURE: https://meazure.us/

MediaBrew: https://www.mediabrew.io/

Oveit, Inc.: https://oveit.com/

**Penhole, Inc.**: https://penhole.com/
**Perflo**: https://www.perflo.co/
**Perks**: https://www.getperks.io/
**RealQuik**: https://realquik.io/
**Simbiosis**: https://simbiosis.team/
**Streams.live**: https://streams.live/
**Vitro Technology Corporation**: https://vitro.io/
**Voxable**: https://www.voxable.io/
**Yes Love, Inc.**: https://yesloveweddings.com/

# Resources

Clean Clause, Inc. sells delicious sparkling yerba mate, and I order it by the case. The company donates 50% of its profits to recovery programs. If you live in an area where they are distributed, apply to the company for a "clean kickstarts" scholarship if you are ready to get sober. cleancause.com/pages/apply-for-scholarship

The 12-step approach of Alcoholics Anonymous and Narcotics Anonymous doesn't resonate with everyone. Some people might like the Smart Recovery program better, since it allows moderation. Look for a meeting here: https://www.smartrecovery.org/community/calendar.php

Even if you've never been diagnosed with a mental illness, if you're having a rough time transitioning you may need some temporary help. It's comforting to know you're not alone. National Alliance on Mental Illness offers support to people with anxiety, depression, or other challenges. https://www.nami.org/Home

Meditation has helped millions find equanimity, inner peace, and peak performance. My go-to is the Headspace App. I also have the Calm app and The Tapping Solution.

Though I consider ADD my superpower and have taught myself many workarounds over the years, if you think you or a family member may have ADD, I highly recommend my friend John Ratey's books and videos. You can read about him on http://www.johnratey.com/.

We are all born alone and we die alone, but while we're living our lives we don't have to suffer alone. Ask a friend of family member for help if you need it. And if you know someone who is vulnerable, take the first step and reach out. We're all in this together.

If you're a startup, these books are helpful:

*Growing a Business* by Paul Hawken
*Startup Success: Funding the Early Stages of Your Company* by Gordon Daugherty

# Acknowledgements

This is usually the most boring part of a book, isn't it? A bunch of names you probably don't know, who did something to make the book possible. As a first-time author, I'm going to say a few words here about the people who deserve some credit for how this book turned out, so if you like it, they should take a bow, too.

First, my parents. How can anyone say they accomplished anything in life without the help of (or challenges presented to them by) the people who raised them? I was blessed with two wonderful human beings who inspired me, sacrificed for me, and encouraged me. Thank you, mom and dad.

Shoutout to my editors: Olivia Buehl, who read a truly horrible first draft and gave me a few comments; Xandra Castleton, who read a slightly better one and gave me some notes; and my good friend—the editor who rescued me by taking the book apart and putting it back together again—Sheila Buckmaster. You're the best, Sheila.

I'm grateful to my early readers, who gave me brutally honest feedback. When you're trying to get feedback on a company, a product, or a book, it helps a lot more to have someone say "fix this, fix that, I don't get it" rather than "it's great, I love it." And the later-stage "early readers" who liked it enough to give me a blurb, MWAH!

My best friends since we met at NBC in 1982, Shelley Ross and Andrea Ambandos, have seen me through divorce, widowhood, and all of my reinventions of self and career. And my newer bestie, Wendy Makenna, invited me to start a company with her in 2013. What a ride that was! The sisters we discover as adults can be as close as family, and these women are.

The brilliant, visionary and always entertaining Daniel Morrell. put me on the CHANT team and let me peek behind the curtains in Hollywood. Thank you, Dan.

The dozens of startup founders who have inspired me with their courage and vision have my endless gratitude. Working in startups gives me hope. Every day, women and men are taking big risks to make things that improve our lives. We owe them a lot.

A special thanks to my former husband, Doug, who bravely allowed me to tell the truth of our story as I saw it. I'm so happy you married Agniezcka, and you're the father of two teenaged boys today. Congratulations, and bless you, Doug.